D0935532

Garth Brooks

Titles in the People in the News series include:

PEOPLE
IN THE NEWS

Garth
Brooks

by Jack L. Roberts

Lucent Books, San Diego, CA

No part of this book may be reproduced or used in any form or by any means, electrical, mechanical, or otherwise, including, but not limited to, photocopy, recording, or any information storage and retrieval system, without prior written permission from the publisher.

Library of Congress Cataloging-in-Publication Data

Roberts, Jack L.
    Garth Brooks / Jack L. Roberts.
        p. cm. — (People in the news)
    Includes bibliographical references (p.   ) and index.
    Summary: Discusses the life, career, and success of recording artist Garth Brooks, who is credited with helping to introduce country music to the mainstream.
    ISBN 1-56006-549-4 (lib. bdg. : alk. paper)
    1. Brooks, Garth Juvenile literature. 2. Country musicians—United States Biography Juvenile literature. [1. Brooks, Garth. 2. Musicians. 3. Country music.] I. Title. II. Series: People in the news (San Diego, Calif.)
ML3930.B855R63   2000
782.421642'092—dc21
[B]   99-31951
                                                                                                    CIP

Copyright © 2000 by Lucent Books, Inc.
P.O. Box 289011
San Diego, CA 92198-9011
Printed in the U.S.A.

Table of Contents

Foreword

FAME AND CELEBRITY are alluring. People are drawn to those who walk in fame's spotlight, whether they are known for great accomplishments or for notorious deeds. The lives of the famous pique public interest and attract attention, perhaps because their experiences seem in some ways so different from, yet in other ways so similar to, our own.

Newspapers, magazines, and television regularly capitalize on this fascination with celebrity by running profiles of famous people. For example, television programs such as *Entertainment Tonight* devote all of their programming to stories about entertainment and entertainers. Magazines such as *People* fill their pages with stories of the private lives of famous people. Even newspapers, newsmagazines, and television news frequently delve into the lives of well-known personalities. Despite the number of articles and programs, few provide more than a superficial glimpse at their subjects.

Lucent's People in the News series offers young readers a deeper look into the lives of today's newsmakers, the influences that have shaped them, and the impact they have had in their fields of endeavor and on other people's lives. The subjects of the series hail from many disciplines and walks of life. They include authors, musicians, athletes, political leaders, entertainers, entrepreneurs, and others who have made a mark on modern life and who, in many cases, will continue to do so for years to come.

These biographies are more than factual chronicles. Each book emphasizes the contributions, accomplishments, or deeds that have brought fame or notoriety to the individual and shows how that person has influenced modern life. Authors portray their subjects in a realistic, unsentimental light. For example, Bill Gates—the cofounder and chief executive officer of the software giant Microsoft—has been instrumental in making personal computers the most vital tool of the modern age. Few dispute his business savvy, his perseverance, or his technical expertise, yet critics say he is ruthless in his dealings with competitors and driven more by his desire to maintain Microsoft's dominance in the computer industry than by an interest in furthering technology.

In these books, young readers will encounter inspiring stories about real people who achieved success despite enormous obstacles. Oprah Winfrey—the most powerful, most watched, and wealthiest woman on television today—spent the first six years of her life in the care of her grandparents while her unwed mother sought work and a better life elsewhere. Her adolescence was colored by promiscuity, pregnancy at age fourteen, rape, and sexual abuse.

Each author documents and supports his or her work with an array of primary and secondary source quotations taken from diaries, letters, speeches, and interviews. All quotes are footnoted to show readers exactly how and where biographers derive their information and provide guidance for further research. The quotations enliven the text by giving readers eyewitness views of the life and accomplishments of each person covered in the People in the News series.

In addition, each book in the series includes photographs, annotated bibliographies, timelines, and comprehensive indexes. For both the casual reader and the student researcher, the People in the News series offers insight into the lives of today's newsmakers—people who shape the way we live, work, and play in the modern age.

The King of Country Music

Country music superstar Garth Brooks says he remembers the exact moment when he decided he wanted to be a country singer. It was the summer after he had graduated from high school and before he went away to college. He was in the car with his dad, driving to a store, and the disk jockey on the radio suddenly said, "Here comes a new guy from Texas. I think you're gonna like his sound."

The new guy was George Strait, and he totally blew Garth Brooks away. "From that minute on," Brooks says, "I knew that I wanted to be just like him."[1]

It took a while for Brooks to achieve the goal he set for himself that day, but people who knew Brooks back then say they aren't surprised he became popular. He was always an entertaining performer.

But no one—not even his most ardent fans—could have

After hearing George Strait sing on the radio, Garth Brooks decided he wanted to become a country music singer.

predicted the phenomenal success he has achieved since his early days in Oklahoma. By 1999 Brooks had sold more than 70 million albums, more than any other solo recording artist in history.

The movie Urban Cowboy *sparked an interest in country music that expanded its appeal beyond rural southerners.*

Garth Brooks has done more for country music than simply sell a lot of records, however. He has introduced country music to mainstream America, helping to make country music popular not only with people of all ages but also with people in all parts of the country—from Bangor, Maine, to Bakersfield, California.

For years America's country music had been dismissed by many people as music by and for rural southerners. Then, in 1980 (the same year Brooks graduated from high school), there was a surge of interest in country music among a wider audience as a result of the movie *Urban Cowboy*, starring John Travolta. But within five years, country-and-western music's popularity had waned once again.

In 1989 Garth Brooks entered the country music scene and completely changed its image. As *Rolling Stone* magazine put it in 1993, Garth Brooks "transformed country from a sleepy musical backwater into one of the most commercially vital sounds on the contemporary scene."[2]

The numbers suggest the dimension of the change. In 1989, the year Brooks released his first album, there were only seven major country-and-western record companies located in Nashville, Tennessee, the home of country-and-western music. By the mid-1990s, there were twenty-six. At the same time, the number of country-and-western music radio stations nationwide also dramatically increased—from fifteen hundred in the early 1980s to twenty-five hundred by 1992. More importantly, sales of country music records skyrocketed. In 1970 country album sales amounted to about $100 million a year. By 1995 sales had increased to $2 billion with more than 60 million Americans tuning into country music stations every week.

In his book *Dreaming Out Loud: Garth Brooks, Wynonna Judd, Wade Hayes, and the Changing Face of Nashville*, Bruce Feiler explains why he believes so many Americans have developed an interest in country music.

> Economic success has brought Americans closer together. Fifty years ago, when the Grand Ole Opry was at its peak (and baby boomers were just being born), America was still largely rural. Only 46 percent of Americans had phones; 10 percent had TVs. Today, by contrast, half of all Americans live in suburbs and most have access to cable TV, the Internet, and that modern town square: the outlet mall. These changes have affected popular taste. As Americans grew older and more comfortable, they grew increasingly interested in the old-fashioned values of their rural past.[3]

Garth Brooks, the leader of the country music pack, has had an almost unbelievable impact on the music business. That impact is exemplified in the number of records he sold in 1995 alone. That year, according to Feiler,

> fifteen albums went gold [meaning they sold 500,000 copies], twenty-six went platinum [1 million copies], five reached 2 million, four reached 3 million, one passed 7 million, and one, Garth Brooks' *No Fences*, topped 10 million units.[4]

No wonder that as early as 1992 *People* magazine had crowned Brooks "the New King of Country."

Part of the reason for Garth Brooks's astounding success is that, from the very beginning, he appealed not only to traditional country music fans but also to the younger people who grew up listening to pop music and rock and roll. As the editor of *Billboard* magazine explained in 1991,

The Mainstreaming of Country Music

Country music was once considered to be only for rural southerners. Today, country music is popular everywhere and with almost everyone from the suburbs to the inner city. In his book *Dreaming Out Loud: Garth Brooks, Wynonna Judd, Wade Hayes, and the Changing Face of Nashville*, Bruce Feiler explains how country music has suddenly become mainstream, appealing to young and old alike.

> While most pop [music] focused on sex, drugs and rebellion, country spun yarns of love, heartache, family ties and midlife renewal. Not only aging baby boomers, but also their children, are espousing these values. The emphasis is on developing a moral code, one based on genuine emotion, not ironic detachment. Fifteen-year-old LeAnn Rimes sings about angels, God and achieving big dreams. Mindy McCready, 21, wonders whether her boyfriend will still love her if she chooses not to sleep with him. And in one of the biggest songs of recent years, "Strawberry Wine," Deana Carter recalls life on the farm—not picking okra, but falling in love. "He was working through college on my grandpa's farm / I was thirsting for knowledge and he had a car." It's Mayberry R.F.D. for the '90s. The true appeal of country music is these stories. And the moral of these stories is simple, if counterrevolutionary: Family values are sexy—not only for over-the-hill hippies who had their fun, but also for young people.

Today's generation buys Garth the way they'd buy Sting or Jesus Jones or Tom Petty, because they like him, not because he's country. And it's everywhere—in West Coast beach towns, Buffalo, and New York City. Country artists see themselves on a much bigger landscape.[5]

Another reason many people believe Brooks has been so successful is that he has always been willing to stand up for what he believes in. He often expresses those beliefs in his music, even when they are controversial. According to Curtis W. Ellison in his 1995 book *Country Music Culture: From Hard Times to Heaven*,

In six record albums between 1989 and early 1994 and in numerous appearances on cable and network television as well as in print media, [Brooks] embraced the causes of hungry children, exploited fans, homosexuality, war, environmental concern, domestic violence, foreclosures, civil rights, and date rape.[6]

Perhaps *TV Guide* writer Mark Lasswell explained Brooks's broad appeal best when he said,

> He's a country star who vamps like a rock 'n' roller, a singer who can go heartfelt ("The River") as well as flat-out raucous ("American Honky-Tonk Bar Association"). On-stage he comes off as a hell-raiser who'd apologize profusely for any broken furniture. He's pulled off the toughest act in showbiz: being all things to all people.[7]

Brooks himself is characteristically modest about his role in the popularity of country music, explaining the success of country music this way: "I think it's filled with real people. Singing about real life. As simple as it sounds, there it is."[8]

A Country Music Enigma

To many people in the music business, Brooks is an enigma. He's been called everything from a hip hillbilly to the artist of

Country Music in the 1990s

By the early 1990s Garth Brooks was single-handedly changing the perceptions of country music. He probably best explained those changes in the opening segment of his first NBC special, "This Is Garth Brooks," which was filmed in 1991 and aired on January 17, 1992. Edward Morris excerpts that opening in his book *Garth Brooks: Platinum Cowboy:*

> Hi. I'm Garth Brooks. . . . For the next hour, I'm gonna try to show you what a Garth Brooks is. For a little head start, I'm fortunate enough to play country music for a living. I'm from the state of Oklahoma, and—wait! [Brooks thrusts out his palm in mock alarm, begging you just to hear him out for a moment.] Where are you going? Oh, the country music thing, huh? I know what you're thinking: dull . . . [quick cut to a shot of Brooks clang-clang-clanging the neck of his guitar across a set of cymbals] boring . . . [Brooks crouches over his guitar and scooters himself across the stage on one foot] old hat . . . [an apparently deranged Brooks stands onstage, spastically hurling sprays of bottled water high into the air] kind of like watching paint dry . . . [two guitars collide midair and explode into a shower of wooden splinters]. Well, all I've got to say is, Welcome to the Nineties!

the decade; a sensitive poet and a wild showman.

From very early in Brooks's career, there were critics who said his music wasn't really country—that it was pop. But Brooks would always dismiss such comments as nonsense. Maybe his music wasn't traditional country—traditional, at least, in the sense of Hank Williams or Merle Haggard—but it was still country.

Brooks's onstage antics also undoubtedly contributed to his success. His act was something country-and-western fans had never seen before. Whether swinging from rope ladders or smashing guitars, Garth Brooks

Brooks's onstage antics, such as swinging from ropes and smashing guitars, were something country-and-western fans had never seen before.

was more like Mick Jagger than Hank Williams. As one observer writes, "His shows were an eye-popping mixture of honky-tonk raucousness and arena rock pyrotechnics that coaxed even die-hard country music haters to call their friends and declare, 'If he's the captain, I'm playing on his team.'"[9]

The Offstage Brooks

Offstage, Brooks is known for being extremely polite. He exudes "aw-shucks" modesty. For example, in 1998, having sold some 70 million albums, Brooks told a reporter,

> With the numbers stuff, you have to take it with a grain of salt. Yeah, you feel proud, but the true guy in you has to say, "Come on, you're not really on the level of the Beatles." For me, as a fan, the Beatles, Michael Jackson . . . Elvis Presley . . . James Taylor, Billy Joel and 100 more guys are on a level Garth will never get to cause I'm such a huge fan of these people.[10]

People describe Brooks as being sincere and straightforward, even vulnerable. He knows how to laugh at himself, and he does not take himself too seriously. Once, when asked if he was ever going to make a movie, Brooks laughed and said that he didn't think Hollywood had a place for a guy with as many chins as he had.

According to Karen Schoemer, writing for *Newsweek*, "Brooks works triple-overtime to make sure he fulfills what his fans want him to be: a kindhearted Christian with solid family values. A Wrangler-clad Middle American with a pizza paunch. A reliable, regular guy."[11] Despite this nice-guy exterior, there has always been a fighter inside—a fierce competitor who was determined to win at all costs.

And win he has. By 1999 Brooks had sold more record albums than any other solo recording artist in history, including Michael Jackson and Elvis Presley, and won countless music awards, including the Country Music Association Entertainer of the Year Award four times.

It's been a long journey since 1985, the year Brooks first arrived in Nashville. He arrived there a brash young man expecting instant stardom and thinking he would see his name on every water tower in town. It wasn't, of course.

Yet today, Garth Brooks is recognized and loved around the world. He's a phenomenal success. And if he ever doubts it, all he has to do is return to his hometown of Yukon, Oklahoma. There, on top of a water tower, in bold letters, is the name *Garth Brooks*.

Chapter 1

An Uncertain Beginning

THE GARTH BROOKS story begins in Oklahoma in 1962. It was there, in the city of Tulsa, that Troyal Garth Brooks was born on February 7.

Garth was the youngest child in a family that consisted of six children. His father, Troyal, had one son, Mike, from a previous marriage, and Garth's mother, Colleen, had two sons, Jim and Jerry, and one daughter, Betsy, from her previous marriage. Together, Troyal and Colleen had a son they named Kelly in 1961, and a year later they had Garth, the baby of the family.

Four years after Garth was born, the tightly knit family moved to the small town of Yukon, Oklahoma, fifteen miles from Oklahoma City. Founded

The six Brooks children tried to outdo each other with stories and antics in an effort to be center of attention.

in 1891 with a population of eighty-one residents, Yukon has since become a thriving community of more than forty thousand. According to Brooks, it was a great place to grow up, a place where people were easygoing and down to earth.

Garth's father worked as an engineer for Unocal, an oil company located outside of Oklahoma City. He had been a marine in the Korean War and was a strict disciplinarian, but he was also a very caring and loving family man. Garth once described his father this way:

> If I could wrap my dad up in two words, it would be thundering tenderness. He's a man with the shortest temper I ever saw, and at the same time he's got the biggest heart. Some of the greatest conflicts are not between two people but between one person and himself. He knows what's right and he doesn't have any tolerance for what isn't right but at the same time he is so forgiving. I learned from him [to be] thankful for what you got and treat people like you want to be treated. My dad drilled that into my head all my life. We're a lot alike in that way.[12]

Brooks and his father were close, even though Brooks did not always listen to his father's advice. Years later Brooks paid his dad a great compliment when he would say that he wished he had listened to his father more when he was growing up.

The Brooks family did not have a lot of money—Garth's sister, Betsy, says they were absolutely poor—but they always seemed to have a good time. Once a week they would have "Funny Night," when all six kids would try to outdo each other with their amusing stories and antics.

A Love of Music

Besides providing their children with an outlet for their desire to be center stage, the elder Brookses instilled a love of music, particularly country music. Brooks grew up listening to such old-time country-and-western singers as Johnny Horton and Merle Haggard.

Garth's father picked the guitar and sang, mostly just for fun, but his mother had actually had a brief professional career as a country music singer in the 1950s, recording under the name Colleen Carroll. She performed with a country-and-western singer named Red Foley on his television show, *Ozark Mountain Jubilee.* She had also recorded a few songs. But after her children were born, she gave up show business in order to raise her family.

Garth grew up listening to country-and-western singers like Merle Haggard.

As Garth grew older, he heard stories about his mother's short-lived professional career and felt sorry that she had given it up. Today, friends say that one reason he decided to go into show business was to carry on the tradition that his mother had started.

Brooks credits both his mother and father for his interest in music and his success. He says he inherited two very different but important qualities from his parents:

> My mom gave me the limitless feeling of dreaming. Mom can be standing on a bridge that is burning like hell and she'll say: "Well, this bridge'll hold up. I'll just walk right off here." She had the never-dying hope and faith. My dad worked two jobs, had six kids and gave them all an opportunity to go to college—he gave me reality. . . . [He] also gave me the push for perfection.[13]

A Protected Childhood

As a young boy, Garth loved sports and was playing softball even in kindergarten. As he grew older, he became an accomplished athlete. A few years later, he would turn his athletic ability into a college scholarship.

Garth was always a well-mannered youngster. His third grade teacher, in fact, remembers that she "never had any discipline problems with Garth. The only problem I had was that I couldn't keep all the little girls away from [him]."[14]

Despite his popularity with girls, though, Brooks says he did not date until he was sixteen years old. Part of the reason was that he was very protected as a child and even as a young teenager. For example, he was not allowed to go out of the yard unless he got permission first. He finally had his first real date when he was sixteen.

But Brooks didn't seem to mind that his family was so strict. "Everything that was cool to me was going on inside my house," he once said in an interview with *Rolling Stone* magazine.

> My sister was singing, my mom was singing, my dad was playing guitar. My dad was with us in the back yard every night teaching us about football, about baseball, more importantly, teaching us about being team players, finding that competition is great, but competition within yourself is the best thing.[15]

Brooks now confesses, however, that for a long time being a good sport was not a topic he understood very well. He was simply too competitive, despite his father's advice.

The Center of Attention

Despite being a sheltered child, Garth always liked to be the center of attention. His sister, Betsy, remembers that as a kid Garth was always trying to get attention. "Garth was a ham," she told *People* magazine in 1991. "He'd do anything for the spotlight or for laughs."[16]

Although Garth was athletic and popular, he was never an outstanding student. He has often joked that his favorite subjects were gym and lunch. But he did excel at sports. In high school, he played both baseball and football and dreamed of being a professional athlete. "I had a vision of every athletic heroism in the world," he says, "from hitting a home run in the World Series to the winning touchdown pass."[17]

While he was in high school, Garth's dream was to become a professional athlete.

Despite his early exposure to country-and-western music, Brooks says he was not into music very much until he was fourteen years old. By then, he was a huge fan of the rock group KISS. When Garth was seventeen years old, he learned to play the guitar. He joined a band called the Nye, and even had his first paying job as a singer at Shotgun's Pizza Parlor.

At about this same time, Garth attended a concert starring the rock group Queen, known for their wild and theatrical stage antics. Suddenly, for the first time, he started thinking seriously about a career in music, but like many teens about to graduate from high school, he wasn't sure what, exactly, he wanted to do with himself.

In 1980, at the age of eighteen, Garth graduated from Yukon High School. That summer, Brooks heard George Strait sing "Unwound." Something about Strait and that song affected Brooks to the bottom of his soul. "I became a George wannabe and imitator for the next seven years,"[18] Brooks later told *People* magazine.

Years later, Brooks still professes his admiration and respect for Strait—both the singer and the man. He feels that Strait, who is

Yukon, Oklahoma: Home of Garth Brooks

In January 1891 a man named A. N. Spencer filed property deeds for some land overlooking the North Canadian River, directly west of Oklahoma City. Soon afterwards, the post office opened, and by April of that year, the little farming community had a population of eighty-one people. Since then, Yukon has grown to over forty thousand, but it is perhaps best known as the home of country music star Garth Brooks. But Brooks wasn't the first celebrity from Yukon, Oklahoma. In the 1950s, Yukon native Dale Robertson became a famous actor, playing mostly cowboys.

very family oriented, is a role model that anyone should be proud to emulate. Strait is known to be a genuine and sincere individual, a dedicated family man, and an all-around nice person. In fact, Strait has often been called "the Gentleman of Country Music."

College Life

Brooks had enrolled at Oklahoma State University (OSU) at Stillwater. He had decided on OSU for three reasons. One was that it was a short two-hour drive from home. The second was that his brother, Kelly, was already a student there, so he would have someone he knew and trusted to help him adjust to college life. Finally, Brooks had gotten a track scholarship to OSU. At six foot one and 225 pounds, Brooks could hurl the javelin two hundred feet. Nevertheless, he always maintained that he was never really that good as a track-and-field athlete. In fact, he later claimed that the only way anyone knew he was on the track team was that he wore a uniform that said he was.

Brooks loved sports competition not only for the competition itself but also for the underlying psychology. He once said about competition, "I love to see how winners react. I love to see how the people that didn't come in first react. And I truly believe the only losers are those who chose not to play the game. Whatever game that might be." [19]

Brooks majored in advertising and marketing at OSU, even though he wasn't sure what he wanted to do after he graduated. During this time, he would play the acoustic guitar, mostly in his room or at various informal gigs around campus, and he would write songs that would entertain his friends.

Brooks started imagining what it would be like to be a country singer. He often talked about it with his roommate, Ty England, who later became a member of Brooks's band. England was also a guitar player, and the two college roommates started sitting up late at night playing their guitars and fantasizing about their future as a singing duo. But, as England remembers it, suddenly it wasn't just a fantasy to Brooks.

> We would sit in those bunk beds at night and we would talk about, man what if we could be a Jones and Haggard. You know what if that's going to be us someday. And it was a real "what if" to me; [but] it was a "how to" for Garth. And . . . a love of music is what got it all started.[20]

When Brooks was a junior at OSU, he met his future wife, Sandy Mahr, at a bar called Tumbleweeds where Brooks was a part-time bouncer. His job was to keep the female customers out of trouble by breaking up any fights.

It was at Oklahoma State that Garth met Sandy Mahr, who would eventually become his wife.

One night, hearing a commotion in the women's restroom, Brooks went in to investigate. Mahr was having a fight with the jealous ex-girlfriend of the man she was currently dating. Brooks broke up the fight and escorted Mahr out of the bar. But from that moment he was hooked on the beautiful and determined young woman. Soon Brooks and Mahr, who was also a student at Oklahoma State, were dating, and not too much later they were officially a couple. Today, Brooks gives Sandy and her willingness to say what she thinks a great deal of credit for his success. "Sandy's a woman who's every bit a lady," he says, "but she don't take nothin' off nobody—especially me. I owe everything I have to God and her." [21]

Although Brooks had found some direction for his personal life, he still needed to decide where he was headed otherwise. In his senior year at OSU, Brooks failed to make the Big Eight Conference finals in track and field. At the time, he was devastated. His coach gave him some wise and even prophetic advice: He told Brooks that he could now get on with what was important in life.

"What the hell could that be?" [22] Garth remembers thinking. He—and the rest of the world—would soon find out.

Chapter 2

From Yukon to Nashville

BY THE TIME Brooks was a senior in college, he had made up his mind about one thing: He was going to Nashville to become a country singer, no matter what anyone else thought. In fact, he was even ready to drop out of college to pursue his dream. But when he told his mother he was leaving for Nashville, she begged him not to go. "I cried," she recalls. "I said, 'I want you to get a real job. That's why we've sent you to college.'"[23]

After graduating from OSU, Garth left home to follow his dream in Nashville. He returned to Yukon twenty-four hours later.

Brooks relented and promised her that he would stay in Stillwater and finish his last semester at Oklahoma State University. Although he had been an average student through-out his college years, in December 1984 he graduated with a de-gree in marketing. Still, he lacked firm plans for his future.

During his last two years in college, Brooks had been per-forming in a number of honky-tonk joints around Stillwater, in-cluding a bar called Willie's as well as at Tumbleweeds, the bar where he had met Sandy Mahr. He also had worked part-time as a sales clerk at a local store, DuPree Sports Equipment.

Despite whatever other career possibilities might have been available, Brooks's heart was set on becoming a country singer. By the spring of 1985, Brooks knew he had to try his luck in Nashville. He approached his mother once again and asked to have her bless-ing to go to Nashville, also known as Music City, but she wouldn't give it to him. She was scared for him. She knew firsthand how tough the entertainment business was. "I said, 'No, but I'll pray for you,'" she recalls. "I never gave him my blessing. Entertainment was so hard on a woman, I assumed it would be that way for a man."[24]

A Humbling Experience

Brooks was determined to follow his dream. So he packed his bags, said good-bye to Mahr and his band members, and headed for Nashville, convinced he was going to take the city by storm. It would take less than twenty-four hours for a heavy dose of reality to hit him. "I came to Nashville thinking that opportu-nity just hung on trees," Brooks told writer Tony Byworth. "That was really naive. I don't want to call it stupid. It [was] just naive."[25]

On the day Brooks arrived in Nashville, he went to see Merlin Littlefield, the associate director of the American Society of Composers, Authors, and Publishers (ASCAP), an organiza-tion that collects royalties for its songwriter members. Littlefield had seen many other young people come to Nashville hoping to become country music stars; he had also seen just as many head for home without achieving that dream. So Littlefield gave the bad news to Brooks straight. He told the eager young musician that the odds were stacked against him. As Brooks remembers it,

[Littlefield] sat me down and told me that my two choices were to starve as a songwriter or go out as an artist and starve with eight other people. While I was with Merlin, there was this call that so-and-so was in the lobby. He told me, "Great, you're going to see one of the greatest writers in Nashville." So this guy comes in and tells Merlin he's having trouble paying off a $500 loan. When he left, I said, "Merlin, that guy was kidding you, wasn't he?" He said, "No, that's really how it is." I said, "Merlin, I make that in a week back home." And he said, "Go back home." I walked away from there hating Merlin's guts, but every day I thank God that he said what he said. Nashville was not the place for me then.[26]

The advice shocked Brooks. He suddenly felt defeated even before he began. Within twenty-four hours, Brooks returned home to Yukon, feeling totally dejected:

I thought [Nashville] was like Oz, and you came here and all your prayers were answered. I thought you'd come here, flip open your guitar case, play a song, and

Although Brooks's first attempt at Nashville was unsuccessful, he would soon take the world by storm.

someone would hand you a million bucks, tell you, "Come into the studio right quick, son, we got ten songs we want you to cut," you cut them that day, go back home and people would be asking you for your autograph that night. And as much as it sounds like I'm exaggerating, I'm not. I really felt that way.[27]

Even though he was devastated by what he learned during that first trip to Nashville, today Brooks says that the trip was a great learning experience, something he wouldn't trade for anything in the world. He needed the cold hard facts laid out for him, and they were.

Back Home in Oklahoma

After he returned to Oklahoma, Brooks says he hid out at his parents' house for three weeks without talking with or seeing any of his old friends. According to Mahr, Brooks was truly heartbroken and felt like a failure. The only career goal he had really set for himself must have looked impossible.

Brooks finally realized that he had to face his friends and tell them the truth about what happened in Nashville. He knew, as he put it, that "lyin' just ain't gonna work."[28] He returned to Stillwater and got his old job back at DuPree Sports Equipment. He also returned to the clubs where he had been playing in and around Stillwater and asked if he could come back to play there. All of the club managers said yes and never asked any questions or made him feel bad about not "making it" in Nashville.

Nashville, Tennessee: Home of Country Music

It's no wonder that Nashville, Tennessee, is known as Music City. It was there, in 1864, that the first country song was published. But it wasn't until the *Grand Ole Opry* (originally known as radio station WSM's *Barn Dance*) began broadcasting weekly radio shows that Nashville suddenly became known throughout the world for its music industry. Today, in addition to being known as Music City, Nashville is often called "the Athens of the South," mainly for its dedication to the fine arts. There is even a replica of the ancient Greek Parthenon in a city park, which today serves as an art museum.

In fact, according to Matt O'Meilia, the drummer in Brooks's band at that time, almost everyone welcomed him back home as if he were a hero:

> No one razzed him or told him he was a big loser—not to his face, anyway. When Garth returned to the microstage at Willie's, the Wednesday night club greeted him like a war hero. But as he resumed playing those same old songs and watching those same old faces inhaling cig after cig after cig, he sensed his Nashville dream evaporating in the warmth and security of local-hero status. So, right there on the smallest stage in the world, Garth devised a plan to sever his umbilical cord from Willie's and return to Nashville.[29]

Brooks resumed playing in bands around Stillwater, and in March 1986 he formed a new band called Santa Fe.

A New Wife

Two months later, on May 24, 1986, Garth Brooks and Sandy Mahr were married. At the time, Brooks was a reluctant groom. Getting married wasn't something he particularly wanted to do. He loved Sandy, but he was also afraid of being tied down.

As a result, Brooks admits that for the first two years of his married life, things were a little rough. He even occasionally wondered if he and Sandy were meant for each other. He often thought about a former girlfriend, thinking that maybe he should have married her instead. Today, he knows differently: "Just the realization that what you have is the best for you, and the best you could ever have in your lifetime. It sure makes you sleep well at night."[30]

Brooks wrote about those feelings in a song called "Unanswered Prayers," which is on his second album, *No Fences*. In that song, he sings about a man who runs into an old high school flame and recalls how he used to pray to God that they would one day be together. But the man in the song realizes that he and his former girlfriend really have little in common. He also realizes how wonderful his life is with his wife. He concludes that unanswered prayers are sometimes better than those that are answered.

A Second Trip to Nashville

By the summer of 1986 Brooks had become a minor celebrity in and around Oklahoma City and Stillwater. He was clearly the star of Santa Fe, a true showman who loved the attention. As his former drummer Matt O'Meilia recalls, Brooks

> seemed to recharge his batteries with every show. He couldn't get enough of performing. When he wasn't performing, he was looking forward to the next performance. . . . [He] was burning with music fever like no one I had ever seen. Even at that early stage of the band's career, we all began to see that he would probably one day enjoy some degree of national success with or without the rest of us.[31]

Brooks loved performing for an audience, but he could see that the local music scene offered him limited opportunity for national stardom.

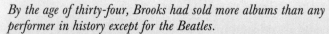

By the age of thirty-four, Brooks had sold more albums than any performer in history except for the Beatles.

Around this time, Brooks began talking about going to Nashville again to try to get a recording contract; in May 1987 he and one of the Santa Fe band members, David Jed Lindsey, headed to Nashville. As he often said at that time, "If you're gonna play in the big leagues, you've gotta be where they're swingin' the bats."[32]

When Brooks and Lindsey first arrived in Nashville, they stayed with a friend named Bob Childers, a Stillwater songwriter who had moved to Nashville a year earlier. Childers was friends with a country-and-western songwriter from Florence, Alabama, named Stephanie Brown. Brown would later introduce Brooks to Bob Doyle, who, with Pam Lewis, would become Brooks's manager.

Brooks and Lindsey soon rented a house of their own in Hendersonville, located just off of Music Row, one of the main streets in Nashville where country music producers have their offices. They then called the rest of the band members in Stillwater and told them to come to Nashville. Sandy also joined Brooks in Nashville.

This time, Brooks was sure he and his band, Santa Fe, were on the right track. They were going to make it big in Nashville. Within a month, however, the band broke up. Most of the members returned to Stillwater, some because they were homesick, others because they doubted the band would ever succeed. Brooks held on, though, determined to be a success despite the odds against that ever happening.

The Making of a Star

Those odds were tremendous. To become an international star takes talent, for sure. And Brooks had the talent. But it also takes luck and some other special qualities. In his book *Garth Brooks: The Road out of Santa Fe*, O'Meilia tries to explain the odds of anyone—even with talent and luck—becoming the kind of international celebrity that Garth Brooks has become:

> How likely is it for a complete unknown to land a major record contract that fast in Music City, USA? About as likely as hitting the jackpot on the first try on every slot

machine in Las Vegas. Because of the sheer lightning speed of Garth's rise to the top, it's hard to believe that he didn't know somebody with serious Nashville leverage before he moved out there. . . . But even if Garth knew every entertainment executive in America from the time he was in kindergarten, that still would not explain how he, at the age of only thirty-four, had already sold more albums than anyone in history except the Beatles. No person or group of people can arrange that kind of success. A combination of so many things— talent, passion, intelligence, timing, luck, genes, and determination—made it all possible.[33]

Trisha Yearwood

Born on September 19, 1964, Trisha Yearwood grew up in Monticello, Georgia, listening to all kinds of music, from country to rock and roll. In 1985 she moved to Nashville to go to college, where she soon became a demo singer for country songwriters—that is, she performed the vocals for new songs that had not yet been recorded. She later sang backup on Garth Brooks's album *No Fences*. Today, Yearwood is the only female country artist whose first four albums (*Trisha Yearwood, Hearts in Armor, The Song Remembers When,* and *Thinkin' About You*) have all reached platinum status or above. Yearwood has toured the world, performed with symphony orchestras, and appeared in a major motion picture and on the television sitcom *Ellen*. She even performed for President Bill Clinton's 1996 inauguration. Yearwood is committed to education, and she often speaks on college campuses to discuss the importance of education in achieving personal goals and to explain the business side of music.

The only female country artist whose first four albums reached platinum status, Trisha Yearwood once sang backup for Garth Brooks.

After his band broke up, Brooks sang background vocals for George Jones (pictured with Brooks) to earn extra money.

After the band broke up, Brooks kept writing songs while he and Sandy both worked at a boot shop in Nashville. He also kept performing. To earn extra money, he even sang background vocals for country music star George Jones in a song called "I Don't Need Your Rockin' Chair."

Brooks's new managers, Doyle and Lewis, began pitching Brooks to every major record label in Nashville, but no one showed any interest. In fact, they all seemed to have a fairly harsh opinion about this young Oklahoman. Author Bruce Feiler writes that "all seven major record labels promptly rejected Garth. He had an undistinguished voice, they said, was a mediocre songwriter, and wasn't very attractive to boot." [34]

By the end of 1987, Brooks was once again beginning to feel like a failure. He was frustrated and depressed. One day he and Sandy were sitting in their car in a parking lot of a fire station in Hendersonville. As Brooks recalls that day, "[I was] beating my head as hard as I could because I had snapped, and Sandy [was] screaming at me to quit. I was crying, she was crying. I calmed down, and we went back home." [35] Brooks told Sandy that maybe they should return home to Oklahoma for a while. But this time Sandy put her foot down. "I'm not makin' this trip every year," she told him. "Either we're diggin' in, or we're goin' home for good." [36]

Fortunately for him and his many fans, Brooks decided to dig in.

Chapter 3

A "Cultural Phenomenon"

IN HIS BOOK *Garth Brooks: The Road out of Santa Fe*, drummer Matt O'Meilia describes Brooks's early determination to make it big in the music business:

> Garth used to tell people he'd be big. They'd laugh, of course, but not because they thought he lacked talent or sincerity. For most normal, eight-to-five folk, fame is simply alien to reality. On the surface, there's no great secret to Garth's fame. He is a driven man. Everything he has accomplished he wanted badly. He worked hard. I've never known anyone in any walk of life who was so completely hell-bent on making it to the top. That's why few who know him were surprised Garth entered the spotlight. But when his fame spilled over into the realm of cultural phenomenon, everyone—including Garth—dropped their jaws in disbelief.[37]

The real beginning of this "cultural phenomenon" known as Garth Brooks happened on the night of May 11, 1988. That night Brooks performed at the Bluebird Cafe, just minutes from Music Row in Nashville. The Bluebird Cafe was a place where songwriters and singers, both those unknown and those established, would go to try out new material.

On that fateful night in May, Lynn Shults, a music executive with Capitol Records, was in the audience. His job at that time was to find new acts for the record label, and what he found that night was Garth Brooks.

Actually, it wasn't the first time Shults had heard Brooks sing. A month earlier Bob Doyle and Pam Lewis, Brooks's managers, had set up an appointment for Brooks to sing for Shults and another Capitol executive named Jim Fogelsong. Neither one was particularly impressed with this country singer from Oklahoma, and they said so. But they had not seen Brooks perform live—until that night in May. "I don't remember what the first song was [that he sang]," Shults said years later, "but I'm pretty sure the second one was 'If Tomorrow Never Comes.' Garth blew me away." [38]

Austin Gardner, a songwriter with Brooks in the early days, remembers that night and what happened after Brooks's performance:

It wasn't like everybody stood up and cheered. You've got to remember that the only people in the club were music industry executives and other songwriters. These were no ordinary fans in the room. The applause was real strong, but at the same time it was like you could hear brain cells clicking together—because you had like three or four heads of different labels, eight different producers, and five [other] people in the room. Nobody wanted to jump up on their chairs and start screaming because somebody else might sign him. [39]

It was not until music executives from Capitol Records saw Brooks perform live that he was offered a recording contract.

A Recording Contract

Shults's instinct and experience told him that Brooks could be big. So that night, Shults shook hands with Brooks, guaranteeing him a contract with Capitol Records; on June 17, 1988, that contract was signed. It meant that Capitol Records intended to release and promote a record in the near future by this young unknown performer. And if Brooks was unknown to the music business, so too was that business unknown to him.

Brooks could not believe it. He was thrilled, of course. But he was also scared to death. He wanted so badly to record something that people would really like. He wanted his friends and his family back in Yukon, Oklahoma, to be proud of him and his accomplishments and to like his first song.

Ten months later, on March 25, 1989, Brooks released his first single. It was called "Much Too Young (to Feel This Damn Old)," and it debuted at number ninety-four on *Billboard* magazine's country singles chart. The song's theme was fairly typical of country music: It was about a man who is sad because his wife has left him, even though he understands why she left.

A month later Brooks passed another milestone when his first album, called simply *Garth Brooks*, made its debut. "The first album is always a big one for any artist," Brooks says, "and I, without trying to sound egotistical, I'm very proud of my first one."[40]

On that album were four songs that made it onto *Billboard's* top ten chart, including "If Tomorrow Never Comes," "Much Too Young (to Feel This Damn Old)," "Not Counting on You," and "The Dance." These hits would make Garth Brooks a country music star almost overnight and the album itself went on to become the best-selling country album of the 1980s.

The Nashville Music Business

Soon after Garth Brooks signed his contract with Capitol Records in 1988, a music executive named Jimmy Bowen became the company's new president. Described by some of his critics as a self-centered yet energetic producer, Bowen was a seasoned veteran of the music industry, having successfully run five other record labels prior to coming to Capitol.

When Bowen took over Capitol, Garth Brooks had already released his first single and was quickly being recognized as Capitol's rising young country star. Bowen saw Brooks as a true phenomenon, a performer unlike any other the nation had seen in many years. "Elvis Presley was the first time I saw this kind of

Garth Brooks has been compared to Elvis Presley and the Beatles —musical phenomenons of their time.

reaction [to a new performer]," Bowen told *Time* magazine in 1992. "Then I saw it again with the Beatles. And now I see it with Garth Brooks. When you turn on millions of people in a short period of time, that's called a phenomenon."[41]

Bowen and Brooks got along just fine for the first few years. But as time went on, the two began to argue about many different aspects of Brooks's career, including what songs he should record and when they should be released. Gradually, the two grew farther and farther apart. Some of Brooks's business associates say that Brooks always resented Bowen because when Bowen first arrived at Capitol, he fired Lynn Shults and Jimmy Fogelsong, the two men who had given Brooks his start.

According to Bowen, however, his problem with Brooks was that the singer was unable to allow others to do their jobs:

Garth was turning into a control freak, wrapped up in details his people should have been handling. His explosive success and new fame—he externalized it as "the GB thing"—

had distracted him. I sensed a dark, almost self-destructive aura around him.[42]

A Strategy for Success

During this time, Brooks's managers laid out a strategy that would help build Brooks's career. Brooks was a dynamite performer in concert, so they decided to capitalize on his concert appeal by having him be the opening act for bigger name stars, such as Reba McEntire. But there were other aspects to the strategy as well. As

Reba McEntire

Country music singer Reba McEntire has sold more than 40 million records during her career. Yet in college, she studied classical violin and piano. She was born on a seven thousand-acre ranch in Chockie, Oklahoma, on March 28, 1955. She got her start in country music as a teenager in the 1970s, when she and her sister, Susie, and her brother, Pake, formed a group called the Singing McEntires. In 1974 she sang "The Star Spangled Banner" at the National Rodeo Finals in Oklahoma, where country singer Red Steagall heard her and helped her get a recording contract. Her first single, "I Don't Want to Be a One-Night Stand," was released in 1976. But it wasn't until 1984, when she started to manage her own career, that things began to happen for her. That year, the Country Music Association (CMA) named McEntire female singer of the year. Today, McEntire is the best-selling female country singer of all time. She has won two Grammy Awards, an unprecedented four CMA female vocalist of the year honors, and the CMA's prestigious Entertainer of the Year Award.

Reba McEntire is the best-selling female country singer of all time.

Curtis W. Ellison explains in his book, *Country Music Culture: From Hard Times to Heaven,*

> The Brooks strategy was to isolate his image as a distinctive voice, promote him on cable television through music video, emphasize the experiential impact of his live performances, and sell key songs as a focal point of controversy in country music culture.[43]

It was a strategy that would help propel the young performer into the musical celebrity stratosphere.

Pam Lewis remembers the excitement, energy, and enthusiasm of those early days:

> Garth made me believe in his dream so convincingly that I wanted to take it to the world. If you had told me after the first year that he was the Second Messiah, I would have believed you. He was so magical. He was such a great coach. He was such a great people motivator—of his band, of his staff, of my staff. People loved him.[44]

What a Concert Is like for Garth Brooks

People loved Garth Brooks for many reasons, not the least of which was the total energy he put into his concerts. In an interview with Robyn Adair on Country 105 radio station in Calgary, Canada, Brooks attempted to explain what a concert performance was like for him, even though he admitted that his description might make people think, "This guy's nuts":

> The people's screams, and what they do is almost like an oxygen that you breath and then you just send it right back out. It gets on this loop and it starts getting "frensic" and that's when you start to feel things . . . the end of your third finger, your small toe. And you're probably the most alive that you've ever felt and you just glow. You have all the confidence in the world . . . it's giving and taking, it's gentle, it's hard, frantic . . . it's pleasing and all this building toward this wonderful thing and you look at each other and say, "I can't take it anymore and you know you've done it right."[45]

The energy that Garth puts into his concerts has made fans out of millions of people.

Harsh Realities of the Business

Events were moving fast for the young performer. He learned some of the perks a music star could expect. And, just as quickly, Brooks learned about some of the harsh realities of the entertainment business. For example, early in his career he had granted an interview to a national magazine in exchange for the promise of his picture on the cover. As it turned out, the magazine put a small photo of him on the cover with a much larger photo devoted to a different story. When Brooks saw the magazine, he hit the ceiling:

> The reason I agreed to spend all that time with those people is they agreed to give me the cover, which could help sell some records, I suppose. So basically what this magazine does is say, "Now that I've got what I want, screw you, Garth, and you can't do anything about it." My managers tell me to forget it, that if I get the press against me it's all over. But I wasn't raised to take that sitting down. You have to stand up and take your swings.[46]

Dealing with the press was only one aspect of the music business that Brooks had to learn the hard way.

Life on the Road

Soon after the release of their first album in April 1989, Brooks and his band went on the road, performing in country music concerts around the nation. The band included his sister, Betsy, as his bassist, and Ty England, his old college roommate, as guitarist. Brooks's brother Kelly worked as the tour manager. "I surrounded myself with people who knew me long before I happened," Brooks says. "So if I start acting different, man, they'll square me in a minute."[47]

Yet, at the same time, Brooks realized that his life was changing dramatically and in many ways he was not living in the real world. Early in his career, during an April 1993 interview with *Rolling Stone* magazine, Brooks explained why his life on the road and as a celebrity was not "real life":

You wake up at one or two in the afternoon, and you see a guy you've known since the second grade, and he says: "Hey man, here's your schedule. I've already called these people and set up everything. You wanna go get something to eat?" So we go, and if it's a busy place, he runs in and gets it for me, and we sit and eat and talk. Then, the next guy comes looking for you, and it's a guy you've known all your life—your brother. He says: "Okay, here's the scoop for tonight. We've got this percentage here and this percentage here. We've come up short with this money and come up over with this money." And then he goes: "There's dinner, you wanna go eat?" So I go eat with him. Then you get ready to go onstage. It's a thing of ours [that] before we go onstage, all the band members get together, we hold hands and try and say something that's funny or inspirational. But in that handshake, I look up, and there's a woman that I've known all my life, my sister [bassist Betsy Smittle]. I look at a guy who was one of my college roommates [guitarist] Ty England. And when we finish, my sister

Ty England

When he was growing up in Oklahoma, Ty England used to strum country songs on his grandfather's guitar, singing the songs of Hank Williams and other country greats of the day. Later, in high school, he joined the school's band, but it wasn't until he went to college at Oklahoma State University at Stillwater that he began to play the acoustic guitar. During that period, he met a fellow student named Garth Brooks, and the two became fast friends. A few years later, England got a call from Brooks inviting him to come to Nashville, where Brooks had signed a recording contract. For the next seven years, England played acoustic guitar and sang harmonies in Garth Brooks concerts throughout the country, but he never lost his desire to be a solo performer. In 1995 he got the chance to go out on his own with the album *Two Ways to Fall*. In an entry that appears in the *Encyclopedia of Popular Music*, England said, "More than anything else, Garth taught me that every fan is important. They are the reasons you're out there. And if those fans could know one thing about me, I'd want them to know that I'm here for the right reason—a lifelong love for music."

comes up, and gives me a high-five, says, "Hey, man, I had a great time tonight. You wanna go eat?" I say, "Sure." And I go back to sleep and the next day it's the same. This is not real life.[48]

Adoring Fans

As the band toured, Brooks developed an ever-growing following of adoring fans. Many of these, of course, were women who would do anything to get close to their idol, including throwing their undergarments at him while he was onstage. Brooks loved the attention, and to make matters worse, he admits today that he liked to flirt.

The fact that he was away from home so much strained his relationship with Sandy, who wasn't traveling with him at that time. Rumors got back to Sandy about Brooks's flirtations with his female fans. Finally, Sandy discovered that her husband was having an affair. In November 1989, during a phone call just before Brooks was to go onstage in a concert, Sandy gave her husband an ultimatum. She told him she was prepared to leave him unless he was ready to make some immediate changes in his behavior. According to Sandy, "I told him my bags were packed, my plane ticket's bought, and I'm gone. You come home and we'll talk, on my turf, eye to eye."[49]

Later that night, onstage in Cape Girardeau, Missouri, Brooks choked up during the chorus of the melancholy song "If Tomorrow Never Comes." In the song, a man wonders whether the woman he loves would know how much he truly cared for her if he were to suddenly die. As he began to sing the chorus of the song, Brooks choked up and had to stop the band to regain his composure. As he recalls,

> I just broke down, stopped the band, tried to keep play-ing, but they didn't know what to do. They looked at me like what are we supposed to do, and I asked them to stop. Then I explained to the crowd what was going on, and I asked for a second chance. I still to this day re-member looking back and Mike Palmer is our drummer. Looking back and the kid was playing, but his face was just soaking wet. He was crying his eyes out, trying to keep a beat. It was a real emotional moment for all of us. Cause we're all married, and we all go through these things.[50]

Peter Kinder, a music critic at the time for the *Southeast Missourian*, was at the concert that night. In his review the next day, he had this to say about that dramatic moment:

> This relative newcomer to stardom strode out and played for 20 minutes, managing to establish rather a good rap-port with the audience, most of whom had come to see the other two performers. He was able to accomplish this de-spite a persistent hoarseness, especially evident in his speaking voice. Brooks opened with "We Bury the Hatchet But Leave the Handle Stickin Out," which was followed by his current hit with its amusing lyrics, "I'm Much Too Young to Feel This Damn Old" [sic]. Brooks exhibited an-other, far more debilitating problem as he seemed near tears, overcome by a never-explained emotional malady. This became particularly acute as Brooks launched into that heart-tugging ballad of love for the lady in his life, "If

Tomorrow Never Comes." Some 45 seconds into the song, Brooks startled the crowd by stopping his band, falling silent, and then speaking of the "hell" of being on the road, of his love for the woman back home, and how some "bad things are going on." This was as specific as he got. Upon regaining composure, he asked of an empathetic and appreciative crowd, "Could I try again?" and proceeded through a workmanlike version that the crowd loved. After two more songs, Brooks departed to a standing ovation from half the crowd, telling a puzzled audience that he hoped they might see him on another evening, one that was "not so sad."[51]

Even today Brooks says that "If Tomorrow Never Comes" is probably one of the most emotional and moving songs he will probably ever sing. He considers it one of his signature songs—that is, a song for which he is well known and sings frequently in concert.

A Reconciliation

Garth returned home after his concert in Missouri, begging Sandy not to leave him. The reconciliation took a while because Sandy had been hurt badly.

> I wanted Garth to feel my pain. He had hurt me so bad. I had wasted two years of my life is how I felt. I'd been the perfect little wife who thought everything was hunky-dory. The hardest thing was to keep from beating the holy s— outta Garth at the sight of him. He was ashamed, embarrassed, and it was written all over his face. He broke down like a baby. He was on his knees, more or less beggin' me. "I'll change. Anything. You name it, I'll do it."[52]

Sandy finally agreed to take Brooks back mainly, she later said, because she realized that the affair had not really meant that her husband did not love her. "Garth has always been a very sexual person," Sandy told *People* magazine. "It was his ego: proving he could look out, point, and conquer. What made it

Life on the road proved hard for Garth, whose marriage to Sandy was put in jeopardy.

easier to cope with was that it wasn't someone special. It didn't mean anything."[53]

Today Brooks seems almost ashamed and certainly embarrassed when he admits his mistakes back then. "I was a spoiled ass," he says flatly. "Responsibility, commitment was not my game."[54]

Performing, of course, was his game. And he did it better than almost anyone else. He knew that what he wanted was success and fame as a country singer, and he was on his way to achieving both.

Chapter 4

The New Nashville Sound

B<small>Y THE EARLY</small> 1990s everyone, it seems, was talking about the new Nashville sound. According to *Time* magazine, this new sound captured "music's mainstream with a nourishing mix of tradition, down-home showmanship and up-to-date songs for grownups."[55] And no musician epitomized that sound better than Garth Brooks.

But it wasn't just Brooks's unique sound that drew people to him, it was also his stage presence—his often outrageous on-stage performance. Country singer Reba McEntire remembers when Brooks was first getting started in 1990:

> He was so outlandish, so far beyond anything anybody did on stage. I was watching him and everybody's watching him saying what is this guy doing out here. I looked at them and I said, he's gonna be a big star. People like that.[56]

People liked that, indeed. In fact, several generations of people liked that. Most importantly, there were the baby boomers, the generation of adults born between 1946 and 1961. As Priscilla Painton put it in 1992, "By their sheer demographic weight, the nation's 76 million baby boomers continue to determine America's musical preferences. And what America currently prefers is country."[57]

Then there were the suburban teenagers and the twenty-somethings. They, too, liked country's new style. "Country also appeals now to listeners/viewers/buyers who are younger, more musically eclectic, and more geographically diverse than ever before,"[58] reported Edward Morris in *Billboard* magazine.

Brooks's onstage presence has made fans out of several generations of people —from baby boomers to suburban teens.

To meet the increased demand for country music, new record companies sprang up in Nashville seemingly overnight. In 1988, for example, the year Garth Brooks signed his first recording contract, there were only seven record labels in Nashville. By the mid-

A New Breed of Country Storytellers

By the early 1990s, the new Nashville sound was attracting not only a new breed of performers but also a whole new generation of fans. In a *Time* magazine article titled "Country Rocks the Boomers," Priscilla Painton explains the differences in the new country singers and their followers.

Country has achieved its new luster without abandoning its heritage; a heritage so stubbornly rooted in storytelling and simple melody that it has never quite left behind the farm in Poor Valley, VA., where a moody lumberman named A. P. Carter and his clan picked up guitars seven decades ago and invented the Carter Scratch. The new wave of country singers is dominated by artists who have succeeded largely on their own terms, consolidating an eclectic mix of contemporary sounds mixed with old-fashioned catches in the throat, tinkles of the mandolin, sugary sobs and vertiginous [inconstant] sweeps of pedal steel guitar. This generation's performers are the first bred on both rock and country who are consciously choosing Nashville. . . . If the baby boomers have discovered country, however, it is not just out of nostalgia. They have looked across the musical landscape and found a cast of artists who are very much like themselves. Today's hot country stars, Garth Brooks foremost among them, are more likely to be college graduates with IRAs than dropouts with prison records. They put Mercedes and Volvos in their videos and refer to wine and cafes as much as beer and honky-tonks. They worry about keeping in shape and in an era of middle class constriction, about keeping ahead. The women sing about their heartbreaks, but they also rejoice in their sexual independence and ponder their opportunities. Both genders extol the virtues of marital longevity.

1990s there were more than a dozen. (And by 1997, that number would grow to more than twenty-five.)

The growth of the country music business was not entirely beneficial, Brooks felt. Many of these companies started turning out records that were not, in Brooks's opinion, true country. Likewise, these records were being made by people who knew hardly anything about country music. As Brooks explains,

We had a lot of people looking at the paper and going, "Hell, if the hillbillies are making money doing this, then surely us fine and proper people can. Hell, I don't know anything about country music, but we can go down there and make us a killing." And they were making fun of country music while they were in it. And I'm sorry, but I really hope those people find another music to go to. I really love people who truly love country music.[59]

Of course, some people accused Brooks himself of being one of those people who were taking advantage of traditional country music. Brooks heard what they were saying but rejected the notion, suggesting that those who make such accusations do so because they do not know him:

> If it's me you're pointing the finger of blame to, then that's your opinion. I'd like to sit down and talk with you about it. I'd love for you to come out to the farm and do a day's work with me and then walk away saying I don't know what country music is, or what it should represent.[60]

"The Dance"

If people accuse Brooks of not understanding country music, perhaps that is because his music attempts to convey slightly more complex messages than the music of other singers and songwriters. For example, in May 1990 Brooks released "The Dance" as a single. It was a song he had recorded on his first album, *Garth Brooks*.

The song's lyrics seem to talk about a broken romance and the pain that it can bring. Yet Brooks says the song is about much more than a love affair that has ended. It's about real life. It's about the fact that it's better to try to achieve one's dreams, even if you don't succeed, than not to try at all.

When it came time to make the video for "The Dance," Brooks wanted to convey that idea in a simple yet dramatic way, and he did so by showing some of the greatest dreamers of the twentieth century—including John F. Kennedy and Martin Luther King Jr.—who paid with their lives for trying to achieve their dreams. In his book *Garth Brooks: Platinum Cowboy,* Edward Morris explains the video:

> Brooks's concept for the video was both simple and masterful. In his mind, "The Dance" was only incidentally a

In the video for "The Dance," Brooks wanted to show the people who paid for their dreams with their lives—John F. Kennedy (far right) and Martin Luther King Jr. (far left).

love song. As he saw it, the song was primarily about risking everything for one's dream. What better way to illustrate this point than by showing a gallery of great dreamers, all of whom had paid the ultimate price— their lives for the dreams?[61]

"The Dance" quickly became Brooks's second number-one hit. It also became one of his favorite songs to perform. The song would prove to be an enduring hit as well: Five years later, *Country Weekly* magazine would name "The Dance" the all-time-best country song. Even greater success, however, lay ahead for Brooks.

No Fences

On August 27, 1990, Brooks released his second album, called *No Fences*. Some music critics say it is the best album he has ever recorded. Brooks himself says it is the people's favorite album.

No Fences is also Brooks's best-selling album. "The number we have sold surprises me to death,"[62] Brooks says. The album went platinum (signifying 1 million copies sold) within two months. By contrast, it had taken his first album nearly a year and a half to be certified platinum. By 1998 the album had sold more than 16 million copies, making it the best-selling country album of all time.

The album included a song that would become Brooks's sixth number-one single. That song was called "The Thunder Rolls." Even though it was a big hit, "The Thunder Rolls" also caused a great deal of controversy.

A Controversial Music Video

In 1991 Brooks released a music video to promote "The Thunder Rolls" that proved highly controversial. In the video, a wife confronts her adulterous husband and a bitter fight erupts, in which the wife is severely beaten. When the man then begins to pursue his daughter up the stairs, the wife pulls out a gun and shoots him. The violence in the video, some critics felt, was offensive.

Two cable television channels—The Nashville Network (TNN) and Country Music Television (CMT)—immediately banned the video. TNN, which reaches 53 million households, refused to show it, saying that "the depiction of domestic violence is excessive and without an acceptable resolution."[63]

In explaining CMT's decision not to air the video, Bob Baker, CMT's director of operations, said: "We are a music channel. We are an entertainment medium. We're not news. We are not social issues. We are not about domestic violence, adultery, and murder."[64]

Both TNN and CMT said at the time, however, that they would have been happy to air the video if Brooks would have included a follow-up announcement about domestic violence and where one could go for help. "If Garth creates a controversial video," said Jerry Bailey, a spokesman for TNN, "he needs to be willing to take responsibility for its social implications."[65]

At first, Brooks considered that request. In fact, he even videotaped a spot in which he looked into the camera and told viewers that if they had ever been a victim of violence there was a number they could call for help. But Brooks changed his mind about including that message on the video, saying that he didn't want people to think he was trying to make money from the issue of domestic violence.

The negative (and, at times, even hostile) reaction to the video stunned and hurt Brooks. "I'm kind of sad that they want to see the good side of real life," he said, "but they want to turn their backs to the bad side."[66] Nevertheless, he took the rejection philosophically. "TNN has standards; Garth Brooks has standards. For some crazy reason, on this occasion the two did not cross,"[67] he said.

Despite the controversy over the video, that fall it received the Video of the Year Award from the Country Music Association. Today, some critics say the controversy over the video for "The Thunder Rolls" was cynically orchestrated to garner more publicity for Garth Brooks. Whatever the truth might be, the controversy generated television and newspaper coverage, which in turn prompted more interest about the song and consequently more sales.

"Friends in Low Places"

Even greater acclaim awaited. A week before *No Fences* was released, Brooks released a single from that album that became, perhaps, the song most people associate with Garth Brooks. It was called "Friends in Low Places." This song not only became one of the biggest hits of his career, it also became another of his signature songs.

The same month that "Friends in Low Places" was released, Brooks was officially inducted into the *Grand Ole Opry* as its sixty-fifth member. The *Opry*, which began as a radio variety

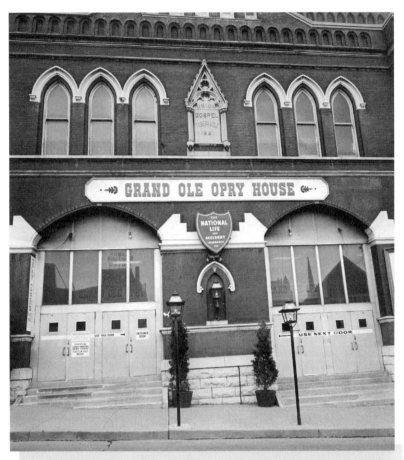

Brooks considers his induction into the Grand Ole Opry *as his greatest achievement.*

program in 1925, is the world's longest-running radio show. Today the show is performed live in front of an audience of up to forty-four hundred fans and is broadcast over dozens of AM stations. Members of the *Grand Ole Opry* are some of the biggest superstars in country music. To become a member, a singer must be invited by the other members.

Brooks considers his induction into the *Grand Ole Opry* his greatest achievement. Soon after becoming a member of this elite country music club, Brooks explained, "It's an award they don't have to give. And even though I can't predict the future, I can't see one higher than that."[68]

Not all music critics were as enamored with Brooks as his fans were, however. In 1992 one music critic had this to say about the country superstar:

His music has enough rock echo to catch the ear of anyone fleeing rap or dance synth on the radio, but it's not aggressive or demanding. It certainly isn't haunting—you'll have to search far afield from Brooks before you glimpse the ghost of Hank Williams—but it is insinuating. Even when he's tackling a fairly serious subject like domestic violence, as in "The Thunder Rolls," it sounds . . . well, nice. Maybe not entirely appropriate, but it sure goes down smooth.[69]

The History of the *Grand Ole Opry*

No other name is more closely associated with country music than the world-famous *Grand Ole Opry*. For more than seventy years, the goal of every young country singer has been to perform on the *Opry*. The story of how the *Grand Ole Opry* became the cornerstone of country music is found on Country.com's "The History of the *Grand Ole Opry*."

On December 25, 1925, a radio program called *Barn Dance* made its debut on station WSM in Nashville, Tennessee. The program featured live mountain music and was an immediate hit. Listeners soon started gathering at the radio station to watch the performers.

The host of the show, a man named George Dewey Hay, insisted on an informal, folksy tone for the show, and he even had his entertainers show up in hayseed costumes and adopt whimsical names like the Fruit Jar Drinkers, the Gully Jumpers, and the Dixie Clod Hoppers.

Barn Dance aired following a radio program of classical music. One night in 1927, *Barn Dance* host George Dewey Hay came on the air and told his listeners, "For the past hour we have been listening to music taken largely from Grand Opera, but from now on we will present 'The Grand Ole Opry.'" The listening audience loved it and the name stuck.

During the next two decades the cast of the *Opry* continued to grow, as did the number of radio stations that broadcast the show. By the early 1950s, The ultimate goal of every country performer was to appear on the *Opry*.

On March 16, 1974, the *Opry* moved from its home in the Ryman Theater in downtown Nashville to a new Opry House at Opryland, a multimillion-dollar entertainment complex on the outskirts of Nashville. The show was broadcast over thirteen hundred radio stations worldwide, marking a milestone in the popularity of country music.

Despite such criticism, by the end of 1991 Brooks was a certified country music star—the biggest on the horizon and getting bigger all the time. He had accumulated seven number-one hits and had released his third album, *Ropin' the Wind,* which became the first country album to ever enter *Billboard*'s pop chart at number one. Garth Brooks was a superstar.

Chapter 5

Contemporary Cowboy

B Y 1992 G ARTH Brooks was making more money than he and his wife, Sandy, could ever spend. In fact, in a list of the top moneymakers in the entertainment industry in 1992, Brooks was number thirteen—and the only country music star on the list. A year later, earning more than $50 million, he moved up to number nine.

Brooks, however, didn't think of himself as anyone special. "I'm still a bum," he told *People* magazine in the fall of 1991.

> I'm no different. I hate to take out the trash and clean my room. Sandy makes me do that stuff. I don't wake up and say, "I cannot believe I am in the middle of all this." I just wake up and say, "You're a bum, go do something worthwhile today."[70]

Yet this so-called bum had made more money in each of the early years of his career, according to author Bruce Feiler, than the entire country music industry had made in 1970. Brooks had achieved his success by creating an unmistakable image in everything he did, whether it was the albums he produced or the concerts he staged. That single image, Feiler says, was that of a contemporary cowboy. "He was humble, courteous, hardworking, and fundamentally all-American. He sang about cowboys. He dressed like Gary Cooper. He wore a hat."[71]

Behind that easy-going middle-America image, however, was also a smart and tough businessman. According to Karen Schoemer, a reporter for *Newsweek,*

Brooks's image as a contemporary cowboy has made him over $50 million.

When the tape recorder goes off, a different person starts to emerge. He talks about the 150-acre homestead he bought for his parents in Oklahoma after the S&L [savings-and-loan] crisis of the 80s, when foreclosed land could be scooped up for a fraction of its value. He discusses share prices on the London Stock Exchange and the optimum conditions for corporate takeovers. It's not unusual for a star of Brooks's magnitude to be packing the business savvy of a Fortune 500 CEO. But Brooks puts an inordinate amount of energy into keeping his off-hours business self hidden from his fans. He treats his enormous wealth—and the brains that achieved it—as guilty secrets.[72]

Even still, no one can deny that a great deal of Brooks's success comes simply from the talent and energy he brings to his work. From the beginning, he was flashy and gimmicky, putting on outrageous high-energy concerts unlike any country music concert anyone had ever seen—wild and frenzied one minute, then gentle and tender the next, then crazy and explosive once again. "When my people leave the auditorium," Brooks once told a reporter, "I want them crawling out. I want them so damn tired. I want their voices gone. I want them to be just like me, wringing wet, just dead. . . . I want to wear my people out."[73]

Music reviewers have always recognized Brooks's unusual, almost hyperkinetic stage presence. As Marjie McGraw reported in the *Saturday Evening Post* in 1992,

> He works the stage like a caged animal, pacing nervously, stopping only to share small, intimate details of his life as they relate to the songs he sings. On stage, he represents nonconformity, escape—helping fans to shed their inhibitions and get in touch with their real feelings—that's what makes him exciting.[74]

Spontaneous Concerts

None of Brooks's shows are choreographed. He likes to keep each concert performance spontaneous and lively, and he also likes the element of surprise. In a biography of Brooks posted on the Internet, the writer relates a story that exemplifies the extent to which Brooks will go to keep his performances fresh. The scene was the final performance of a sold-out concert in Canada:

> It had been a long, exhausting tour and the band was starting to wear down. They knew it. Garth knew it and decided to fix it. Prior to showtime, he called the band together for a pre-game huddle. "I'll pay five hundred dollars in cash to anybody who can knock me down on stage tonight," Garth announced. "Impress you with a guitar lick or what?" someone asked. "No, I mean physically knock me flat on my butt," he said. That got 'em jumpstarted. And all through the night they took their best body slams much to the delight of the Canadians who witnessed it.

When Garth was still standing by the final number, somebody gave the signal and they rushed to center stage, toppling him into a pile of laughing band members. (They split the cash.) It was too close to call as to who loved it best: the audience, the band, or Garth Brooks.[75]

In addition to the dazzling show, fans also respond to the music, whether a heart-tugging ballad or a honky-tonk saloon song. Music critic Robert K. Oermann put it this way:

Brooks never choreographs his concerts, preferring to keep them spontaneous.

He's like yin and yang. Any time you've got somebody who can melt your heart with a ballad, then turn around and dazzle people onstage, you've got a star. The guy does both—he's a sensitive poet and the wild showman—that's the combination that touches people. He's everyman; he's a people's artist, an everyday guy who made it.[76]

"Pop's Pillsbury Cowboy"

Yet this "people's artist" is not to everyone's liking. In 1992 *USA Today* rock critic Edna Gundersen found Brooks and his music bland and uninteresting.

Brooks' safe, approachable songs—pleasant to most, offensive to few—broadened his demographics just as Pat Boone, the Bee Gees and the Monkees prevailed with mass-appeal pablum [blandness] in their day. Pop's Pillsbury cowboy may be elevating country's profile, but he's no musical messiah.[77]

There were other opinions, of course. In response to Gundersen's scathing attack on Brooks and his music, critic Edward Morris wrote a response in *Billboard* magazine:

What most rock critics either don't understand or won't accept as valid are the traditions of civility and self-effacement in country music. Rock seems to revel in "rawness" and posturing, usually mistaking them for wisdom. Country prefers a more measured and restrained approach, even when the subjects are provocative or violent. The elements in Brooks' songs that Gundersen derides as "safe" and "approachable" are absolute virtues to people who prefer not to be lectured to or shouted at. In country music, the singer is always subservient to the song. Brooks knows that and has benefited greatly from that knowledge. It is too bad that he is insufficiently barbaric for Gundersen's tastes. The rest of us can handle his smoothness.[78]

By Brooks's own admission, a song from the heart is what he is all about:

Brooks's View on a Sensitive Subject

In 1992 Garth Brooks created a great deal of controversy with his song "We Shall Be Free." The song, Brooks says, was about relationships between all kinds of people. But the song also seemed to support gay relationships. In an interview in the March 1994 issue of *Interview* magazine, Brooks told reporter Peter Galvin a story that he says explains his feelings about homosexuality.

There's a guy back home that I sincerely love. . . . Rumor has it—and I've never talked to him about it and it really doesn't matter—that he's homosexual. I ran into him one night in a club. I went there with my manager, and he was sitting at the bar, and I went up to say, "Hey." We always hug each other, so I'm hugging him and I'm standing there talking to a bunch of people and he sits down next to me. We're talking and all of a sudden I feel this—what he's done is reached down and grabbed my hand. So we're sitting there actually holding hands at the bar. And there're people watching me, making me feel real uneasy about it. Then, all of a sudden I think: Which is going to bother you more? People seeing you holding this guy's hand, or how he's going to feel if you pull your hand away? Not breaking that guy's heart or insulting him in any way meant so much more to me than anybody's opinion about me. So I just relaxed. Then we went to dinner and it was cool. I thank God that moment happened to me because since then, I've been real cool about that kind of thing.

I'd rather have one song that was from the heart than eight songs that were clever and went to No. 1 on the charts. If I get a song that I feel is on a parallel from my heart to yours, instead of coming from my mouth to your ears, then I think I've got something.[79]

The Chase

On September 22, 1992, Brooks released an album that came from his heart. His fourth album was called *The Chase*. Within a week after the album was released, it was number one on *Billboard*'s top two hundred albums chart and on its top country albums chart.

For Brooks, *The Chase* was a special album. He called it the most personal album he had made, an album that revealed a great deal about who he was as a person. As he explains,

It was recorded at a time in my life that was probably the most trying time of my life. Not the fact that it was a hard time for me. I was just going through a lot of things at this time. Probably the biggest thing was expecting the birth of our first child, Taylor. [I] was also in the business for record renegotiations; we were remodeling our house. And still trying to go through the biggest tour I'd ever been on since *Ropin' the Wind.* . . . So when you hear this album or snippets from it and you hear things that are more, probably, socially oriented as far as concerns of the world. And some things that are a little bit darker, that's probably cause that's where I was at that time. It was a big moment. And I gotta say of the albums I've ever done this one has the best writing on it and probably one that I feel the strongest about. I'm very proud and I love this album.[80]

"We Shall Be Free"

While the album was hugely successful, one of the socially oriented songs on the album, which had been released in August 1992, created more controversy than any other song Garth Brooks has ever recorded. "We Shall Be Free" is a song about equality for all people—for the poor, for people of color, for people of all religions. In it, Brooks sings about his own wish and vision for the world—a world in which there is no poverty, no racial discrimination, and no destruction of the environment.

However, some of Brooks's advisers felt he should not release the song because of one line in which he says that people will be free when they are allowed to love anyone they want. His advisers worried that many of his fans might feel that he was advocating or promoting homosexuality.

Brooks remained adamant about releasing the record because he felt it had an important message. In response to the concern from his advisers, Brooks, who had actually been talking about retiring, simply joked, "I might not have to worry about retiring; my career might be over."[81]

As expected, the song and its presumed message stunned some of Brooks's fans. They claimed he was supporting gay

The song "We Shall Be Free" sparked controversy because the message for equality for all people was taken by some as advocating homosexuality.

rights, and they objected to that. "We lost some fans that followed us very closely,"[82] Brooks told *Interview* magazine in 1994.

As it turned out, "We Shall Be Free" made it only to number twelve on the music charts. It was the first single that Brooks had released that did not make it to the top ten. Some critics say the reason the song wasn't more popular was because it apparently defended homosexuality, and as a result, radio disc jockeys refused to play it. Jimmy Bowen, head of Capitol Records at that time, disagreed. "Radio didn't resist it; they played it for eight or nine weeks. They just didn't get any phone calls for it. People didn't like it."[83]

Brooks told the press that he was very proud of the song and of the message it delivered for all minorities. In an interview with

Overrated Showman?

Not all of the national music critics are fans of Garth Brooks. *USA Today* rock critic Edna Gundersen had few nice things to say about Brooks and his music in a March 1992 article subtitled "Overrated Showman."

A pale and pudgy Oklahoman with an unremarkable voice and a Wonder Bread sound continues to tyrannize pop music. . . . Speaking for the few mystified listeners who haven't been swept away by the Garth tsunami, I say enough already. If some semblance of taste and daring is to be restored to mainstream pop, this hip hillbilly's reign must end. Before the clones come marching in. . . . To suggest Brooks converted rock-soured college students into die-hard country fans puts the cart before the horse. Pop masses flocked only after he eschewed country conventions and played by rock rules. Such MTV-generation strategies as stage theatrics, slick videos and headline-generating controversy boosted Brooks into the stratosphere. Meanwhile, worthier talents like Jimmie Dale Gilmore, Lyle Lovett, and Steve Earle toil in the shadows.

music critics Melinda Newman and Edward Morris in September 1992, Brooks expressed his views about discrimination:

As long as you think the color of skin affects how someone can do their job, as long as you think who someone chooses to sleep with affects how they do their job, it's not a free country, it's an ignorant nation. The fact that homosexuals feel they have to have individual rights is a direct failure of people to realize that we're all human beings. The fact that there is a word "minority" represents a failure that we all realize we're human beings.[84]

Six months after the release of "We Shall Be Free," Brooks was interviewed by Barbara Walters for her television program, *The Barbara Walters Special.* During that interview, Brooks revealed that his sister, Betsy, is a lesbian.

After the program was taped, Brooks's manager, Pam Lewis, thought they should try to get Walters to edit out the remark before the show aired. Brooks refused:

I've lived with that forever. And the thing is, the longer you live with it, the more you realize that it's just another form of people loving one another, so it doesn't become something special to you, something that's extreme or odd to you.[85]

At first, Betsy was very upset. "It put me in a state of panic," she says. "I thought, 'Oh, my God, they're going to blow up the [band's tour] bus or something.' But nothing bad came of it. A lot of good came of it, really. People are a bit more open-minded."[86]

But Brooks believes that the line in the song that upset many people really isn't so much about people dealing with being gay but about people dealing with being themselves:

In that song, I was talking about relationships between all kinds of people—interracial stuff, Jewish people with people from other forms of religion. But all the reviews focused in on gay. It's like, hey, imagine anything and its opposite coming together. Or anything that seems the opposite of how life has been, coming together. It's all about love.[87]

A Family Man

On July 8, 1992, two months before *The Chase* was released, Garth Brooks became a father—an event that affected him

It was on The Barbara Walters Special *that Brooks told viewers that his sister, Betsy, is a lesbian.*

deeply. Brooks and Sandy named the baby girl Taylor Mayne Pearl Brooks. Brooks says she was named after singer James Taylor, the state of Maine (where she was conceived), and the legendary country singer Minnie Pearl.

It had been a difficult pregnancy for Sandy. In fact, when she was four months pregnant she became ill and had to be rushed to the hospital. For a while, the Brookses were afraid they might lose the baby.

During that time, Brooks took four months off from touring in concerts so that he could be with Sandy. He even talked about retiring, even though he was only thirty years old and his popularity was at an all-time high. He certainly did not need any more money; as he told the press, he and Sandy had "50,000 times more money than we could spend in the rest of our lives."[88]

Yet his love for music and for performing kept him going. The excitement of not knowing just how successful he could become may also have played a role in his decision not to retire. "I feel as if I'm a child again," he said at the time, "watching an Oklahoma thunderstorm gather in the distance, anticipating its wonder yet fearing its potential. And loving every minute of it."[89]

A Patriotic Brooks

Indeed, it seemed there was no limit to that potential. On August 31, 1993, Brooks released his fifth album, *In Pieces*. It entered the pop and country charts at number one. That album included the song "American Honky-Tonk Bar Association," which celebrates the virtues of working people and also expresses Brooks's views about patriotism.

As Brooks explains,

I'm a flag-waver. . . . I would like to see the United States as a very patriotic country, a very proud country—but also a country that allows love and freedom of expression, that allows people to pursue whatever in hell they want to pursue, as long as it doesn't offend the rights of others.[90]

It's a theme that Brooks has seemed to always pursue, both in his career and in his personal life.

Chapter 6

The Two Garths

Eᴀʀʟʏ ɪɴ ʜɪs career, Garth Brooks realized that there were really two Garths—the down-home "aw-shucks" Garth, who says
"sir" and "ma'am"; and the tough, competitive, shrewd businessman Garth. In the souvenir program for a 1992 concert
tour, Brooks describes his dual personality:

> Garth is not difficult to understand if you look at him as two
> different people. There's GB the artist and Garth the lazy
> guy just hanging around the house. Here's how the two dif-
> fer: GB likes the view from the edge; Garth hates heights.
> GB loves to try new things; Garth is a meat and potatoes
> kind of guy. GB loves the control, responsibilities and duties
> that come with the road. Garth enjoys being lazy, dreaming,
> and other senseless things that people call foolishness.[91]

Maturity in Business and at Home

By the beginning of 1994, a third Garth Brooks had clearly emerged,
the family man. He had a loving relationship with his wife and a
baby daughter, whom he adored. By all accounts, Brooks the family
man was a happy man. "If I had to trade one yesterday so I could
have one more tomorrow, I don't think I'd do it,"[92] he said.

During the next two years, Brooks and his wife, Sandy, had
two more children, both girls. August Anna was born in 1994,
and Allie Colleen was born in the summer of 1996.

Brooks's daughters had a profound effect on him and on his
attitudes about his career. When he first started out as a singer,
Brooks used to say that performing was the only thing that gave
his life meaning: "The only time I know I'm really alive and

doing something in God's great earth is when I'm in between those speakers and the lights are up and the music is loud. I never want to get down; I never want to get off the stage."[93] But after the birth of his three daughters, Brooks began saying that his first goal in life was to be a father:

> I always thought being a success in the music business was what was going to be the mark that I left. Now I know that those [three] kids will be the greatest mark I could ever hope to achieve. And how they turn out sets the quality of the mark I leave.[94]

Brooks wants his daughters to grow up strong and independent, and he says that if they have inherited any of his or Sandy's traits, they will. He knows how tough the world can be, and he wants his daughters to be prepared for it. In many ways, his feelings are the same as his mother's when she discouraged him from making the trip to Nashville a decade earlier.

Brooks also worries about making sure that his little girls grow up level-headed and unspoiled. But, he confesses,

> It's tough to pick out the normal-little-girl stuff from the spoiled-little-girl stuff. Like when [Taylor] leaves half a sandwich on the plate, I start thinking, "Oh, God, don't let her get used to taking just a bite out of something and think we'll just get some more if it runs out."[95]

Brooks also feels that he learned a lot from his parents about how he wants to raise his own children. Soon after the birth of his first daughter, Brooks explained to news anchor Jane Pauley on *Dateline NBC* that what he felt was most important to give his children was his time and attention:

> I know my mom and dad didn't have money to give their kids. I know that. But the one thing they did have was time and attention. And that made me feel like I was very important to someone. That is what I must give my little girl. The fact that we have millions of dollars means nothing to her.[96]

Brooks says that even though his parents did not have money, they gave him "time and attention" and that made him feel like he was "very important to someone."

Early in 1996, Brooks and his wife decided that for their tenth wedding anniversary, on May 24, they would renew their wedding vows in a second wedding celebration. But when Sandy became pregnant with Allie, the couple decided to postpone their celebration until October.

While there had been some troubles in their marriage, particularly early on, Brooks and Sandy now shared a strong commitment to make their marriage work. Moreover, Brooks had realized how much he really cared for his wife. He says that for the first six years that they had been together, he was too busy focusing on his career to really get to know her. Beyond an emotional attachment, what he discovered when he did was "one of the neatest people I've ever met."[97]

An Open Feud

The deepening of Garth Brooks's relationship with Sandy was not, however, reflected in his relationship with Capitol Records. By 1994 the feud between Brooks and Jimmy Bowen, head of

Capitol Records in Nashville, had intensified. Sales of Brooks's albums had dropped, and Brooks blamed Bowen for the decline. Bowen, in turn, said that Brooks was his own worst enemy. "I can give you fifteen reasons why his sales dropped," Bowen said, "but he can only give you one: me." [98] Sales had dropped, according to Bowen, because Brooks was saying things in his songs that people didn't want to hear and his freshness had faded. His new music was simply not as good, Bowen claimed.

To make matters worse, Brooks and Bowen had become embroiled in a major disagreement over Brooks's new recording contract with Capitol, now called Liberty Records. Brooks wanted total control over his records, including owning the masters, the original recordings from which all other copies are made. He also wanted the right to determine the release dates of his albums and singles, and he wanted an advance on royalties of millions of dollars. He also told Bowen that he wanted 30 percent of the net profits from the sales of his records—the same deal that Michael Jackson had.

No Longer "Mr. Nice Guy"

By the late 1990s many people in Nashville claimed that Garth Brooks had changed. He was no longer the sincere guy he had been when he first came to Nashville. In his book *Dreaming Out Loud: Garth Brooks, Wynonna Judd, Wade Hayes, and the Changing Face of Nashville,* Bruce Feiler offers one explanation why Nashville's music executives turned on Brooks.

> As Garth's career progressed, he began to reveal his alternative side—less genuine, more contrived; less neighborly, more cut-throat. Garth was not the first superstar to make this transition, nor will he be the last. But he was the most visible. And Nashville, sensing the shift from a man who was humble because he felt that way to a man who was humble because he liked how it looked, turned on him. At first this change in attitude toward Garth surprised me. After all, Garth merely did what everyone else on Music Row did (try to make more money; try to manipulate the media), only he did it better. Eventually, I realized there was more to it: Nashville turned on Garth Brooks in part because they didn't like what his transformation said about them. Music Row would like to think of itself as being genuine and pure, while in fact it's often conniving and ruthless, too.

Bowen turned him down flat. "You don't deserve the Michael Jackson deal,"[99] Bowen reportedly told him. Brooks eventually got the contract he wanted, but by then his relationship with Bowen had totally disintegrated. Brooks reportedly decided to try to get Bowen fired. In the summer of 1994, however, Bowen was diagnosed with lymphoma, a form of cancer. In December 1994 he resigned from Liberty Records.

With the departure of Bowen, Scott Hendricks was selected to head Liberty Records, which was renamed Capitol Nashville. Brooks irritated Hendricks and his team from the beginning. "I don't believe in you guys," he told them. "And from what I understand, you're not very good."[100]

Fresh Horses: His Sixth Album

A test of Hendricks and his management team was not long in coming. On November 21, 1995, Brooks released his sixth album, *Fresh Horses*. The music on the album was country through and through, which surprised many fans who were expecting the album to be pop.

Fresh Horses did not do as well as Brooks had hoped, ultimately selling only 4 million copies. Brooks blamed Hendricks for not promoting and marketing the album properly. Brooks claimed that the record company simply gave up on the album after it sold only a couple million copies.

As might be expected, Hendricks disagreed with Brooks, laying the blame directly on Brooks. Hendricks told a reporter from *Newsweek* magazine that *Fresh Horses* failed to do as well as expected because the album simply wasn't one of Brooks's best. "I'm sorry Garth was disappointed with the sales of 'Fresh Horses,'" Hendricks said. "All of us would have loved to have seen sales beyond 4 million, particularly after executing a marketing plan that Garth and his associates signed off on."[101]

Fresh Horses was Brooks's lowest-selling album to date, and the record's disappointing reception left Brooks and Hendricks at odds for the next two years. Finally, in 1997, Hendricks was fired and Pat Quigley, a friend of Brooks's, was named president of Capitol Nashville. There were rumors at the time that Brooks was directly responsible for getting Hendricks and his associates fired.

But, according to Karen Schoemer, a reporter for *Newsweek*, "Brooks claim[ed] he had nothing to do with the firings."[102]

Despite the disappointing sales of *Fresh Horses*, Brooks says that he put a great deal of himself into the album. "It's a huge reflection of myself," he said. "It's the things I enjoy singing about. I got to sing about the band on the road; I got to sing about cowboys, and more importantly, the women who put up with those cowboys."[103]

Fresh Horses, however, includes one song that made musical history. It is the love song "She's Every Woman,"and it debuted on *Billboard's* chart at number thirteen. Five weeks later, it was number one on the chart. No other song had risen that quickly to number one in the history of recorded music. Once again, it seemed that Brooks had the golden touch.

A Different Opinion

Brooks may have a golden touch, but throughout his career he has struggled to keep success from going to his head. Most people who know him say that, despite his success, he's still the nice down-to-earth guy that he always was. "His legendary politeness . . . remains intact," said *TV Guide* writer Mark Lasswell in 1997. "[His] civility seems genuine."[104]

But Brooks knows that being true to oneself can sometimes be tough. "I don't know if I am as sincere as I was," he once said. "I'm hoping when I see myself in the mirror that I'm the same person I was [before I became famous]. But what you see as an outsider might be different."[105] He admits that sincerity sometimes diminishes without one ever knowing it.

Others would agree. They say he's changed from an easygoing, sincere guy to a domineering manipulator. "Spend a week in Nashville," says *Newsweek* writer Karen Schoemer, "and you'll hear executives use these words to describe him: 'monster,' 'egomaniac,' 'bully.' "[106]

Greg Kot, a rock critic for the *Chicago Tribune*, explains the paradox this way:

> [Brooks] connects because he's a safe, apple-cheeked, mother-loving ham. Graying, a touch grizzled and a bit

Throughout his career, Brooks has tried to keep success from going to his head. "I don't know if I am as sincere as I was. . . . I'm hoping . . . I'm the same person I was."

soft around the middle, Brooks could be anyone's next-door neighbor. Only difference is, he's the next-door neighbor who'll skinny-dip at the barbecue and don the lampshade at the Christmas party.[107]

Pam Lewis, one of Brooks's former managers, agrees with those who claim that Brooks has become less genuine. While he may seem totally charming on the outside, she says, "there's a lot of pretense and falseness and veneer. It's insidious."[108]

Bizarre Behavior

Some people say that they first noticed a change in Brooks's personality soon after the release of *Fresh Horses.* On that album is a song called "The Change." The theme of the song is the tragic bombing in Oklahoma City on April 19, 1995.

Brooks wanted every radio station in America to play the song at exactly 9:02 A.M (central standard time) on the anniversary of the bombing. He felt it would be a tribute to the people who were killed in that tragedy. Other people disagreed, accusing Brooks of just being interested in promoting the record. These critics dismissed Brooks's idea as a publicity stunt.

Even more controversial was Brooks's release of a video for "The Change" that upset many people. It consisted entirely of footage of rescue workers at the site of the bombing. "Garth had intended the video to pay tribute to the valor of the rescue workers," author Bruce Feiler explains. "Instead, it was widely viewed, particularly in [Oklahoma], as exploiting the tragedy for his own financial gain."[109]

In addition to the adverse publicity generated by "The Change," in 1996 Brooks did something that many people considered truly bizarre. At the American Music Awards (AMA),

Garth wrote "The Change" as a tribute to the people who were killed in the Oklahoma City bombing.

held at the Shrine Auditorium in Los Angeles, Brooks won the award for favorite artist of the year. He rejected the award, however, and left it standing on the podium in front of him. What was even more strange was that Brooks had won—and accepted—two other awards that same night: one for favorite country album and the other for the favorite male country artist. Why, critics wondered, did he suddenly reject this award? Brooks later explained that he didn't mean any disrespect, but he didn't believe in the concept of an *artist of the year*. Many fans as well as other artists felt he had snubbed the AMA.

By this time, Jimmy Bowen also clearly felt that Brooks's success was going to his head and that Brooks was starting to act like he was infallible. In an interview with country radio personality Ralph Emery, Bowen reportedly said:

> [Brooks] is a guy that sang about "If Tomorrow Never Comes" and "Friends in Low Places" and all these great songs. And in the last year he got to taking himself way too serious. You know, he is not the second coming. He has changed, Ralph, but who wouldn't? It is incredible, but I think the biggest change comes when they get so big and it dawns on them that they are prisoners of it [fame], and they can't go here and there any more. . . . Garth has just become a control freak. He tries to control everything in his life.[110]

Finally, even Brooks's concerts were being criticized. In 1997 Kot wrote about a Brooks concert in which the singer acted like

> an applause junkie playing it humble. After a brisk start, his show bogged down in schtick, with the aw-shucks singer stroking the audience for its enthusiasm, milking its generous shouts and screams for decibels and duration, and joking with his seven-piece band as if they were back on the bar circuit.[111]

"The Thrill Is Gone"

By 1998 many people, particularly in Nashville, were beginning to say that Brooks had changed from a nice easy-going guy to a

FanFair

Each year since 1972, more than twenty thousand country music fans from around the world gather in Nashville, Tennessee, for a giant country music festival called FanFair. Cosponsored by the Country Music Association and the *Grand Ole Opry*, FanFair enables country music fans to meet their favorite artists and attend numerous live country music performances as well as participate in numerous other activities. Although there are always scheduled country music performers throughout the week-long festival, invariably there are surprise appearances by other country stars. For example, at the 1996 FanFair Garth Brooks made an unexpected visit and reportedly signed autographs nonstop for twenty-three hours.

ruthless manipulator. Beverly Keel, a reporter for the *Nashville Scene*, wrote an article titled "The Thrill Is Gone" in which she attempted to explain how Brooks had changed over the years and how people were starting to react to these changes:

These days, the superstar's nickname, "GB," more likely stands for "Garth-bashing"—the most popular Music Row trend since ponytails on middle-aged men. It's hard to say when the cracks first started appearing in his armor of earnestness. Was it when he left the American Music Award or when he outed his sister on Barbara Walters without her permission? It could have been when he announced his "retirement," attacked used CD stores, or told a reporter that he co-wrote most of his songs because he couldn't find any others that were good enough. Brooks should realize that he's neither John Lennon nor John Wayne and that he's become a man the ten-year-old Garth probably wouldn't have liked. Certainly, his contributions are not to be overlooked. His music has touched millions and forever changed the face of country. But unless he refocuses on the music, he's likely to be remembered in the industry not for his successes, but for his shortcomings.[112]

A Sense of Inadequacy

The negative side of Brooks that some people have witnessed may be rooted in his own sense of inadequacy and insecurity. "Brooks seems insecure about life at the summit," one critic has said. "Big-guy handsome at six-foot-one, he worries about his weight and receding hairline and rigidly controls his public image."[113]

Brooks's mother has her own opinion about her son's insecurity. In an interview with author Bruce Feiler, Colleen Brooks offered this point of view:

All males are weak. It doesn't make any difference who they are. It takes Jesus Christ, or a woman, or a parent to make them realize that they're not. I think all males truly want to be a hero. What Garth wants to be is what he thinks every man should be: a person of complete strength, a man of his own mind. I think he'll be perfectly happy with himself when he knows he is a good man. . . . [And] I think he is so close. But I think he doesn't feel it yet. When I talk to him I say, "I'm so proud of you. You're such a good man." And this means

Even with his success, Brooks has insecurities about his weight, his public image, and his career.

all the world to him. What Garth needs to do is stop and say, "It's not what I've done, but who I am," and realize he can only do so much. I don't care who you are—John Wayne or anyone—life only offers you a certain level. Garth's reached it. He just doesn't realize it yet. If I could give him any advice, it would be: "Son, you're there. Be happy and enjoy it." [114]

Certainly, Brooks would agree about being insecure. He has always felt that his popularity would one day disappear. In 1995, soon after the release of *Fresh Horses*, he told *USA Weekend* reporter Jim Sexton how he felt about his success. "I'll feel lucky if they'll let us hang around for another two years," Brooks said. "When it's over for us, it is going to be over. It won't die slowly; it will fall like a rock. So we're out there enjoying it while it is there." [115]

Yet, in the meantime, the criticism has clearly hurt Brooks a great deal. According to his wife, Sandy, he's simply not the tough cowboy he pretends to be:

He'll never be that cowboy. He's just too tender. He wears his heart on his sleeve. He hides it a lot of the time, but he gets hurt. I know he does. This business has hurt him. These people have hurt him. Nashville, especially, has hurt him. And that's the hardest part of all. Look at what he did for them. [116]

Chapter 7

Garth Brooks: The Future of Country Music

GARTH BROOKS'S CONTRIBUTION to country music is indisputable. By the fall of 1997, Brooks had sold more than 62 million records. That made him the top-selling solo artist in U.S. music history, bigger even than Michael Jackson. Yet, suddenly, there were indications that country music's popularity was waning. In 1993, for example, almost 19 percent of all records purchased were country. By 1997 that figure had dropped to about 12 percent.

Some critics blamed the slowdown on the fact that country music songs had all become too similar. Others said that there were far too many country music concerts for even the most diehard country fans to attend.

Still others blamed the decline in the popularity of country-and-western music on the fact that Garth Brooks hadn't released a new album since 1995. What the industry needed, critics said, was the shot in the arm that it could get from a new Garth Brooks album.

That album, observers hoped, would be *Sevens*. The album was so titled, Brooks said, for three reasons. First, it was his seventh album of new music. (He had also released two other albums, including *Beyond the Season*, an album of Christmas music released in 1992; and *The Hits*, released in December 1994). Second, he was born on the seventh of February; and finally, the album would likely push his total sales past 70 million records.

Brooks wanted the people at EMI, the parent company of Capitol Nashville, to handle the marketing of *Sevens*. However, there was a shakeup at EMI, and many of the people who Brooks trusted were fired in the process. As a result, Brooks refused to release the album as originally scheduled on August 7. As *Time* magazine reported, "when Brooks' record label . . . announced in May [1997] that it was . . . getting rid of some of the people [Brooks] had depended on over the years to market his albums, Brooks decided to withhold his new record indefinitely."[117]

Hello New York!

Originally, Brooks had been scheduled to give a free concert in New York City's Central Park on August 7, 1997, which would coincide with the release of *Sevens*. The concert, it was hoped, would help promote sales of the new album. When it became clear that Brooks wasn't going to release *Sevens* on schedule, many of his advisers said there was no real reason to give the free concert. Nevertheless, Brooks insisted that the concert be held anyway. He felt he had a duty to his fans.

As the day of the concert approached, Brooks was nervous. He had never played New York City before. He was also the first country artist (and only the ninth artist overall) to have a major concert in Central Park. He was afraid no one would show up, even though most people were predicting a huge turnout. Brooks said at the time,

> Everybody's predicting huge numbers, but I don't like that—I sure don't want somebody not coming because they think there's going to be too many people there, and then nobody shows up at all. We'll feel lucky no matter how many come out, and we'll play our hearts out [even] if it's only 100.[118]

Brooks had nothing to worry about, though. The concert was a huge success, drawing anywhere from 250,000 people, according to a New York City Police Department estimate, to 900,000, Brooks's own estimate.

Brooks performed a free concert for more than 250,000 people in Central Park.

According to Eric Boehlert, the music critic for *Rolling Stone* magazine, the concert showcased more rock music than country.

All told, during the course of the entire 20-song show, Brooks played just four or five songs that qualified as country in sound or sentiment. Even when he slowed down the concert for a down-home campfire sing-along, Brooks celebrated pop music (yet again) with Don McLean's "American Pie.". . . It wasn't until the final three-song encore that Brooks's show clicked. . . . Brooks's first—and still finest—single, the cowboy lament "Much Too Young (to Feel This Damn Old)," was followed by the equally sweet "If Tomorrow Never Comes."[119]

The Release of *Sevens*

For three months after the successful Central Park concert, Brooks still refused to release *Sevens*. In November 1997, when Scott Hendricks was replaced by Pat Quigley, Brooks finally agreed to release *Sevens* in time for the holidays, when record sellers could expect extra traffic in their stores. The album was officially released on November 25.

Pat Quigley had his work cut out for himself in promoting the new album. He had reportedly claimed that "if he couldn't sell 10 million copies of Sevens, he wasn't doing his job."[120] The album sold 3.4 million copies in the first five weeks but then dropped off dramatically.

Despite the dropoff in sales, the producer of the album, Allen Reynolds, praised it:

> Garth has always impressed me with his passion for music—for life itself—his uncompromising values and his ear for songs. And Sevens is as fine a representation of those qualities as I could have ever hoped for in my heart. Each time I listen to it, I'm moved. This is clearly an artist in his prime.[121]

The reviews of *Sevens* were extremely positive. For example, Reuters News Service critic Gary Graff expressed the opinion of many Brooks fans:

> After all the anticipation, Garth Brooks has finally delivered a pretty damned good album, one that embraces traditional country themes of drinking, suicide, trucks, hell-raising, divorce, infidelity, street-corner religion, and self-determination. . . . It tracks very well, and there are surprises. "Fit For A King," in particular, is the quiet, oddly moving tale of a ragged street-corner preacher. The album ends with a moody World War I evocation, "Belleau Wood." And Brooks veers into pop with the music-hall strains of "When There's No One Around." This is not "No Fences," but nothing ever likely will be. Garth Brooks is ropin' the wind—and everything else.[122]

Although Brooks wrote only six of the fourteen cuts on the album, he says that "many [of the other cuts] are so 'me' that people I work with every day thought I wrote them."[123]

Brooks's favorite song on that album is "Belleau Wood." The song, which speaks poignantly about the universal dream of peace and love among all people, began as a poem in 1988 by a Colorado writer named Joe Henry. Brooks added the music to it and put it as the final cut on *Sevens*. It is, perhaps, a tribute to Henry that Brooks says he always puts his favorite song as the final cut on his albums.

The Promotion of *Sevens*

One controversy arose as a result of Brooks's effort to increase the new album's sales. To help promote *Sevens*, Brooks made a deal with talk show host Oprah Winfrey. In return for Winfrey's promotion of the album on her show every day for a week, Brooks agreed to donate a portion of the proceeds from the album sales to Winfrey's Angel Network charity.

Throughout his career, Brooks has supported many different charities, so his interest in supporting a charity like the Angel Network was not surprising. For example, he had once raised over $4 million for the Ronald McDonald Children's Charities. He had also raised over $1 million for One Voice, the Los

On Charity

Throughout his career, Garth Brooks and his wife have supported many charities, often anonymously. In his book *Garth Brooks: Platinum Cowboy*, Edward Morris tells a story about their gift giving one Sunday afternoon.

Brooks and his wife were at their home watching a United Cerebral Palsy telethon on Channel 2. As the fund-raiser neared the end, it became obvious that the organizers were not getting the level of contributions they had hoped for. This was familiar ground to Brooks, who had appeared on the telethon before, back when he was just building a name. Impulsively, he suggested to Sandy that they drive the few miles to the TV station and make their own pitch for donations. When they got to the station, they were immediately ushered before the cameras. Brooks said he would personally give a dime for every dollar the local viewers pledged. And toward that end, Sandy promptly wrote out a check for twenty-five thousand dollars. There was a quick round of hugs and handshakes, and then—just like the Lone Ranger and Tonto—the Brookses were gone.

Angeles–based organization that assists low-income families with food, shelter, job training, and scholarship opportunities.

But this time, many of Brooks's critics said that the singer's charitable donation came with a catch. Even though the deal raised five hundred thousand dollars for the charity, some critics called it an unabashed ploy to sell records. (And, in fact, sales of Brooks's album during that week pushed *Sevens* from number twenty-four to number four on the charts.)

Once again, the criticism both hurt and puzzled Brooks. As he said at the time,

> It makes no sense to me. If a guy goes out to play golf, and he's trying to shoot the lowest score he can, don't we all want him to? If a guy's driving a car and he wants to get the fastest time he's ever gotten, don't we all want him to do that? And if you're trying to get the music out to as many people as you can, don't people want you to do that? I guess I just never understood it enough to analyze it, why there are people who, when you do something, they immediately jump on it and start smashing the hell out of it. I don't get that. So I probably find myself just steering clear of those people and then looking at my own self in the mirror and say, "Are you doing this for the right reasons?" [124]

It is at times like that when Brooks says he thinks about giving up the country music business altogether. But, on the other hand, he adds that he is a born fighter, and he is not about to let the business get him down. Brooks knows that business well, and he is more than equal to its challenges.

The Product Known as Garth Brooks

As Brooks sees it today, Garth Brooks the singer has become a product; something to market and sell. Maybe that's why he often refers to himself in the third person. But, as he explained to *Newsweek* reporter Karen Schoemer in 1998,

> It's easier for me to talk about Garth than say I. Garth is supposedly the biggest-selling solo act in the United States. I can't say I am. That feels egotistical to me, and

Brooks considers himself a product of the music industry. The president of Capitol Nashville admits, "Of all the products I've worked with, Garth is by far the best."

I hate that feeling. Also, Garth is what you see onstage. Garth is the lighting rig, he's the band and most of all Garth Brooks is the people out there. You gotta admit, the guy would look pretty silly doing all that stuff if no one was reacting. So he's just a reaction of the people."[125]

Even Pat Quigley, the president of Capitol Nashville, who earlier in his career had marketed everything from ski boots to beer, refers to Brooks in those terms. "Of all the products I've worked with," says Quigley, "Garth is by far the best." [126]

By 1997, that "product" was being marketed successfully around the world. In May 1997, for example, Brooks held a concert in Dublin, Ireland, at Crone Park. Brooks elaborates on the concert's success:

> I wasn't sure how the Irish would react. I was amazed. They seemed to know all the songs and could recite the lyrics. Actually, country music and Irish music are surprisingly similar. Especially in the use of the fiddle. The crowds went crazy over [band member] Jimmy Mattingly's playing, and they were so enthusiastic, they mobbed him. It's amazing how people react to the music wherever we go. Whether it's Sydney, Berlin, Madrid, Barcelona, or Dublin, the response is the same that we get at home. [127]

That concert formed the basis for Brooks's fifth NBC television special, "The Garth Brooks Special." Ninety minutes of the two-hour program came from the Dublin concert. Brooks also added other songs, including two duets with his favorite female singers: one with Trisha Yearwood and the other with Susan Ashton.

In January 1998 Garth signed a new recording contract with Capitol that is reportedly worth more than $100 million. Although details of the deal are secret, author Bruce Feiler describes it this way:

> Garth's records are owned by a company he controls called Pearl Records, Inc. (named for Minnie Pearl). Those records are then licensed to Capitol Nashville, which must distribute them on a schedule he determines. Capitol pays for the artwork, which Garth then owns. Capitol, in turn, pays for all marketing and promotion costs. After these costs are deducted, Garth earns upward of 58 percent of the net profit, bringing his take from every album to above $3.00. In addition, in an even rarer move, these terms were retroactive to day one of his career, covering each of the 30 million albums already sold. [128]

That deal reportedly earned Brooks $58 million in 1998 alone.

The History of the Country Music Association

In 1958 a group of country music performers, songwriters, and executives formed the Country Music Association (CMA). The purpose of the organization was to promote country music throughout the world. Today the organization has more than seven thousand members in thirty-one countries. While the CMA has made many contributions to country music over the years, it is perhaps best known for its awards, which are the industry's most highly coveted and preeminent country music awards. The awards, which were first presented in 1967, are presented annually in twelve categories to outstanding country artists, as voted by CMA's membership. Since 1990 Garth Brooks has won eleven CMA awards, including the CMA Entertainer of the Year Award, which he won in 1991, 1992, 1997, and 1998.

By the spring of 1998, Garth Brooks had had fifteen number-one hits and had sold an awesome 67 million albums. He was the best-selling recording artist of the 1990s in any genre and the best-selling country artist of all time.

In the fall of 1998, Brooks once again received the Entertainer of the Year Award from the Country Music Association—the fourth time he had been so honored by the CMA. He accepted the award with his usual modesty, paying homage to the country artist whose music first inspired him:

> If I say this award means more to me this year, it's because we're one year further along in a career where these things aren't supposed to happen anymore. They only happen to the cool people like George Strait who can continue to be the best year after year after year.[129]

Throughout his career, Brooks has achieved most of the goals he has set for himself. But, as 1999 began, there was one goal he had yet to achieve. With more than 107 million albums sold, the Beatles still claimed the record for most albums sold by any performer or group.

Many people believe that Brooks will eventually surpass that figure. But to most of his fans, it is not important whether he surpasses the Beatles. Brooks has already made an extraordinary contribution to American music.

In his book *More Memories,* disk jockey Ralph Emery explains what he believes is Garth Brooks's most important contribution to music, and why Brooks will always be remembered:

> I personally feel that Garth Brooks has done for country music what Elvis Presley did for the popularity of rock 'n' roll, what the Beatles did for new approaches to harmony. Country music has never had a more pronounced, ground-breaking pioneer. He has brought his music to millions who otherwise wouldn't have heard country music. The entire industry is in his debt.[130]

His millions of fans around the world would agree.

Epilogue

Slugger Brooks

On February 18, 1999, thirty-seven-year-old Garth Brooks showed up for spring training with the San Diego Padres. He had decided to take a year off from music, and as far as he was concerned, there was no better way to spend his free time during that year than with San Diego's defending National League champions.

Brooks's primary goal in joining the Padres, however, was not just to play baseball, although he loves the sport (and throughout his career has often talked fondly about how his father taught him to play). His real goal was to raise awareness for the Touch 'Em All Foundation, which Brooks started to raise money for children's charities. The idea behind the nonprofit foundation was that baseball players would pledge dollar amounts based on their performances, and the funds would be matched by entertainers and corporate sponsors.

In announcing the foundation, Brooks said that his dream was that "every swing of the bat, every ball in major league baseball will make kids' lives better. What you hear about in baseball and in all sports is overpaid players. I would love to hear a different tune next year." [131]

No one, of course, expected that Brooks would actually be offered a contract to play with the Padres once spring training ended. But that didn't matter to Brooks, the players, or to the coach. "I might not ever play Carnegie Hall, but that doesn't take away from my passion and my feeling for music," said Padres coach Tim Flannery. "Garth's the same way. He might not ever play major league baseball, but he's got an enormous passion and feeling for the game." [132]

When he took a year off from music, Brooks trained with the San Diego Padres to promote the Touch 'Em All Foundation, a fund-raiser for children's charities.

According to all reports, during that spring training, Brooks worked hard and gave it his all, just as he has done throughout his entire musical career. "He's driven," said Padres general manager Kevin Towers. "He'll hit 200 balls, and then go out with a bucket and pick 'em all up." [133]

That spring, Brooks saved his first three broken bats to give to his daughters: Taylor, 6; August, 4; and Allie, 2. On each, he wrote a message. "They were all a little different," he says, "but the theme was the same: You can do anything." [134] Throughout his career, Garth Brooks has proved just how true that is.

Notes

Introduction: The King of Country Music

1. Quoted in Westwood One Entertainment, "The Garth Brooks Story," Planet Garth, July 4, 1996. www.planetgarth. com/gbstory/gbstory.shtml.
2. Anthony Decurtis, "Ropin' the Whirlwind," *Rolling Stone*, April 1, 1993, p. 31.
3. Bruce Feiler, "Country Music's New Values," *USA Weekend*, April 3–5, 1998. www.usaweekend.com/98_issues/980405/ 980405country_values.html.
4. Feiler, *Dreaming Out Loud: Garth Brooks, Wynonna Judd, Wade Hayes, and the Changing Face of Nashville.* New York: Avon Books, 1998, p. 37.
5. Quoted in Jim Jerome, "The New King of Country," *People*, October 7, 1991, p. 42.
6. Curtis W. Ellison, *Country Music Culture: From Hard Times to Heaven.* Jackson: University Press of Mississippi, 1995, p. 259.
7. Mark Lasswell, "Garth Takes Manhattan," *TV Guide*, August 2, 1997, p. 32.
8. Quoted in America Online interview with Garth Brooks, September 9, 1994. www.westworld.com/~garthbrk/garth9-9. html.
9. Feiler, *Dreaming Out Loud,* p. 6.
10. Quoted in Gary Graff, "Garth Brooks Is Ropin' the Wind and Everything Else," Reuters News Service, May 14, 1998. www.planetgarth.com/gbnews/garth225.shtml.
11. Karen Schoemer, "The World According to Garth," *Newsweek*, March 16, 1998, p. 66.

Chapter 1: An Uncertain Beginning

12. Quoted in Rick Mitchell, *Garth Brooks: One of a Kind, Workin'* *on a Full House*. New York: Simon and Schuster, 1993, p. 17.
13. Quoted in Decurtis, "Ropin' the Whirlwind," p. 32.
14. Quoted in Edward Morris, *Garth Brooks: Platinum Cowboy*. New York: St. Martin's, 1993, p. 25.
15. Decurtis, "Ropin' the Whirlwind," p. 34.
16. Quoted in Jerome, "The New King of Country," p. 41.
17. Quoted in Robert Hillburn, "The Amazing Garth-O-Matic," *Los Angeles Times*, June 28, 1992. www.planetgarth.com/ gbnews/garth055.shtml.
18. Quoted in Jerome, "The New King of Country," p. 44.
19. Quoted in America Online interview with Garth Brooks.
20. Quoted in America Online interview with Garth Brooks.
21. Quoted in Jane Sanderson, "For Garth Brooks, Country Music's Newest Nova, Nashville Proves Sweeter the Second Time Around," *People*, August 1990, p. 92.
22. Quoted in Jerome, "The New King of Country," p. 41.

Chapter 2: From Yukon to Nashville

23. Quoted in Schoemer, "The World According to Garth," p. 70.
24. Quoted in Schoemer, "The World According to Garth," p. 70.
25. Quoted in Morris, *Garth Brooks*, p. 39.
26. Quoted in Morris, *Garth Brooks*, p. 38.
27. Decurtis, "Ropin' the Whirlwind," p. 34.
28. Quoted in Decurtis, "Ropin' the Whirlwind," p. 34.
29. Matt O'Meilia, *Garth Brooks: The Road out of Santa Fe*. Norman: University of Oklahoma Press, 1997, p. 18.
30. Quoted in Westwood One Entertainment, "The Garth Brooks Story."
31. O'Meilia, *Garth Brooks*, p. 87.
32. Quoted in Sanderson, "For Garth Brooks, Country Music's Newest Nova, Nashville Proves Sweeter the Second Time Around," p. 92.
33. O'Meilia, *Garth Brooks*, p. 192.
34. Feiler, *Dreaming Out Loud*, p. 109.
35. Quoted in Elizabeth Bland, "Country Classicists," *Time*, September 24, 1990, p. 92.

36. Quoted in Jay Cocks, "Friends in Low Places," *Time*, March 30, 1992, p. 67.

Chapter 3: A "Cultural Phenomenon"

37. O'Meilia, *Garth Brooks,* p. 5.
38. Quoted in Morris, *Garth Brooks,* p. 59.
39. Quoted in Morris, *Garth Brooks,* p. 61.
40. Quoted in Planet Garth, "The Albums: Garth Brooks." www.planetgarth.com/gbalbums/album-gb.shtml.
41. Quoted in Priscilla Painton, "Country Rocks the Boomers," *Time*, March 30, 1992, p. 63.
42. Quoted in Feiler, *Dreaming Out Loud,* p. 279.
43. Ellison, *Country Music Culture,* p. 218.
44. Quoted in Feiler, *Dreaming Out Loud,* p. 328.
45. Quoted in Country 105, "Featured Artist: Garth Brooks." www.country105.com/artistpast/garth1.html.
46. Quoted in Hillburn, "The Amazing Garth-O-Matic." www.planetgarth.com/gbnews/garth055.shtml.
47. Quoted in Jerome, "The New King of Country," p. 43.
48. Decurtis, "Ropin' the Whirlwind," pp. 32–34.
49. Quoted in Jerome, "The New King of Country," p. 44.
50. Quoted in Westwood One Entertainment, "The Garth Brooks Story."
51. Quoted in Morris, *Garth Brooks*, p. 77.
52. Quoted in Jerome, "The New King of Country," p. 44.
53. Quoted in *People*, "Garth Brooks's Black Eye," May 20, 1991, p. 93.
54. Quoted in Jerome, "The New King of Country," p. 43.

Chapter 4: The New Nashville Sound

55. Cocks, "Friends in Low Places," p. 62.
56. Quoted in Westwood One Entertainment, "The Garth Brooks Story."
57. Painton, "Country Rocks the Boomers," p. 62.
58. Quoted in Morris, *Garth Brooks*, p. 74.
59. Quoted in Country 105, "Featured Artist."
60. Quoted in Country 105, "Featured Artist."
61. Morris, *Garth Brooks*, p. 89.
62. Quoted in Planet Garth, "The Albums: *No Fences*." www.planetgarth.com/gbalbums/album-nf.shtml.

63. Quoted in *People*, "Garth Brooks's Black Eye," p. 93.

64. Quoted in Associated Press (press release), "Two Cable Channels Ban a Country Music Video," May 5, 1991.

65. Quoted in Associated Press (press release), "Two Cable Channels Ban a Country Music Video."

66. Quoted in *People,* "Garth Brooks's Black Eye," p. 93.

67. Quoted in Associated Press (press release), "Two Cable Channels Ban a Country Music Video."

68. Quoted in Westwood One Entertainment, "The Garth Brooks Story."

69. Quoted in Cocks, "Friends in Low Places," p. 67.

Chapter 5: Contemporary Cowboy

70. Quoted in Jerome, "The New King of Country," p. 45.

71. Feiler, *Dreaming Out Loud,* p. 104.

72. Schoemer, "The World According to Garth," p. 66.

73. Quoted in Decurtis, "Ropin' the Whirlwind," p. 35.

74. Marjie McGraw, "Garth Brooks: Hitting 'Em in the Heart," *Saturday Evening Post,* July/August 1992, p. 38.

75. Country.com, "The Artists: Garth Brooks." www.country.com/cgi/redirect.cgi?URL=%2Fgen%2Fmusic%2Fartist%2F garth-brooks.html.

76. McGraw, "Garth Brooks," p. 102.

77. Edna Gundersen, "Garth Brooks: A Breath of Fresh Air or a Pop Intrusion?" *USA Today,* March 12, 1992, p. 13D.

78. Morris, *Garth Brooks,* p. 129.

79. Quoted in McGraw, "Garth Brooks," p. 102.

80. Quoted in Planet Garth, "The Albums: *The Chase.* www.planetgarth.com/gbalbums/album-tc.shtml.

81. Quoted in Melinda Newman and Edward Morris, "Garth Bows Latest (*Billboard*—Last?) Sets," *Billboard,* September 5, 1992. members.billboard.com/archi...ard/archive/92-93/load-6_34.asp.

82. Quoted in Peter Galvin, "Don't Be Fooled by Garth Brooks's Flag-Waving," *Interview,* March 1994, p. 49.

83. Quoted in Ralph Emery with Tom Carter, *More Memories.* New York: G. P. Putnam's Sons, 1993, p. 246.

84. Newman and Morris, "Garth Bows Latest (*Billboard*— Last?) Sets." members.billboard.com/archi...ard/archive/ 92-93/load-6_34.asp.

85. Quoted in Galvin, "Don't Be Fooled by Garth Brooks's Flag-Waving," p. 48.

86. Quoted in Schoemer, "The World According to Garth," p. 70.

87. Quoted in Galvin, "Don't Be Fooled by Garth Brooks's Flag-Waving," p. 48.

88. Quoted in Newman and Morris, "Garth Bows Latest (*Billboard*—Last?) Sets." members.billboard.com/archi... ard/archive/92-93/load-6_34.asp.

89. Quoted in Morris, *Garth Brooks*, p. 160.

90. Quoted in Galvin, "Don't Be Fooled by Garth Brooks's Flag-Waving," p. 49.

Chapter 6: The Two Garths

91. Quoted in Hillburn, "The Amazing Garth-O-Matic." www. planetgarth.com/gbnews/garth055.shtml.

92. Quoted in McGraw, "Garth Brooks," p. 102.

93. Quoted in America Online interview with Garth Brooks.

94. Quoted in America Online interview with Garth Brooks.

95. Quoted in Jim Sexton, "Garth Brooks Goes Global," *USA Weekend*, December 12, 1995, p. 13D.

96. Quoted in Morris, *Garth Brooks*, p. 175.

97. Quoted in McGraw, "Garth Brooks," p. 103.

98. Quoted in Feiler, *Dreaming Out Loud*, p. 280.

99. Quoted in Feiler, *Dreaming Out Loud*, p. 278.

100. Quoted in Feiler, *Dreaming Out Loud*, p. 325.

101. Quoted in Schoemer, "The World According to Garth," p. 68.

102. Schoemer, "The World According to Garth," p. 68.

103. Quoted in Planet Garth, "The Albums: *Fresh Horses*." www.planetgarth.com/gbalbums/album-fh.shtml.

104. Lasswell, "Garth Takes Manhattan," p. 33.

105. Quoted in Decurtis, "Ropin' the Whirlwind," p. 34.

106. Schoemer, "The World According to Garth," p. 66.

107. Greg Kot, "Garth Brooks Rolling Along with Winning Ways," *Chicago Tribune*, October 23, 1997.

108. Quoted in Schoemer, "The World According to Garth," p. 66.
109. Feiler, *Dreaming Out Loud*, p. 187.
110. Quoted in Emery, *More Memories*, p. 246.
111. Kot, "Garth Brooks Rolling Along with Winning Ways."
112. Quoted in Feiler, *Dreaming Out Loud*, p. 332.
113. Quoted in Feiler, *Dreaming Out Loud*, p. 192.
114. Quoted in Feiler, *Dreaming Out Loud*, p. 268.
115. Quoted in Sexton, "Garth Brooks Goes Global," p. 13D.
116. Quoted in Feiler, *Dreaming Out Loud*, p. 332.

Chapter 7: Garth Brooks: The Future of Country Music

117. Christopher John Farley, "Garth Brooks Unplugged," *Time*, August 18, 1997, p. 66.
118. Quoted in Neil Pond, "Garth Takes a Bite of the Big Apple," *Country America*, September 1997.
119. Eric Boehlert, "Garth Brooks: Central Park," *Rolling Stone*, September 18, 1997, p. 47.
120. Schoemer, "The World According to Garth," p. 68.
121. Quoted in Artist Bios and Info, Capitol Records. www.capitol-nashville.com/artistbios/BioGarthBrooks.htm.
122. Graff, "Garth Brooks Is Ropin' the Wind and Everything Else."
123. Quoted in Planet Garth, "The Albums: *Sevens*." www.planetgarth.com/gbalbums/album-seven.shtml.
124. Quoted in Graff, "Garth Brooks Is Ropin' the Wind and Everything Else."
125. Quoted in Schoemer, "The World According to Garth," p. 70.
126. Quoted in Schoemer, "The World According to Garth," p. 70.
127. Quoted in Bob Thomas, "Garth Brooks's TV Special Shows Irish Love for American Country Music," Associated Press, February 27, 1998. www.planetgarth.com/gbnews/garth202.shtml.
128. Feiler, *Dreaming Out Loud*, p. 278.
129. Quoted in Tamara Saviano, Wendy Newcomer, and Deborah Barnes, "A Tale of Two Cities on a Night to Remember," *Country Weekly*, October 13, 1998, p. 26.
130. Emery, *More Memories*, p. 255.

Epilogue: Slugger Brooks

131. Quoted in David Leon Moore, "Brooks a Hit with Padres," *USA Today,* February 26, 1999. www.usatoday.com/sports/ ccovfri.htm.
132. Quoted in Moore, "Brooks a Hit with Padres."
133. Quoted in Moore, "Brooks a Hit with Padres."
134. Quoted in Moore, "Brooks a Hit with Padres."

Important Dates in the Life of Garth Brooks

1962
Troyal Garth Brooks is born in Tulsa, Oklahoma, on February 7.

1980
Graduates from Yukon High School and enrolls in Oklahoma State University at Stillwater.

1985
Makes first trip to Nashville.

1986
In May, marries Sandy Mahr from Owasso, Oklahoma.

1987
Makes second trip to Nashville, this time with Sandy.

1988
In May, performs at the Bluebird Cafe in Nashville, where Capitol executive Lynn Schults promises him a contract; signs a recording contract on June 17 with Capitol Records (later called Liberty Records and then Capitol Nashville).

1989
Releases his first single, "Much Too Young (to Feel This Damn Old)," on March 25; releases his first album, *Garth Brooks*, on April 12; it becomes the best-selling country album of the 1980s.

1990
Releases his second album, *No Fences,* on August 27; it becomes the best-selling country album of all time (16 million copies sold by August 1998).

1991

The Yukon City Council proclaims March 16 "Garth Brooks Day," painting the words *Home of Garth Brooks* atop one of its water towers; releases his third album, *Ropin' the Wind,* on September 10; it becomes the first album to enter both *Billboard's* country and pop charts at number one.

1992

His first daughter, Taylor Mayne Pearl, is born on July 8; releases his fourth album, *The Chase;* it enters the pop and country charts at number one.

1993

In January, sings the National Anthem to over 1 billion people in over eighty-seven countries at the Super Bowl; releases his fifth album, *In Pieces,* on August 31; it enters the pop and country charts at number one.

1994

His second daughter, August Anna, is born.

1995

In November, *Country Weekly* magazine names "The Dance" the all-time-best country song; releases his sixth album, *Fresh Horses,* on November 21.

1996

His third daughter, Allie Colleen, is born; Brooks and Sandy renew their wedding vows on October 26.

1997

Gives free concert in New York City's Central Park on August 7; releases his seventh album, *Sevens,* on November 25; it sells 5 million copies in less than two months.

1998

With nearly 70 million albums sold, Brooks becomes the best-selling American singer of all time.

1999

Joins the San Diego Padres for spring training.

The Albums of Garth Brooks

Garth Brooks
Released April 12, 1989

No Fences
Released August 27, 1990

Ropin' the Wind
Released September 10, 1991

Beyond the Season
Released August 25, 1992

The Chase
Released September 22, 1992

In Pieces
Released August 31, 1993

The Hits
Released December 13, 1994

Fresh Horses
Released November 21, 1995

Sevens
Released November 25, 1997

Awards Received by Garth Brooks

1990

Academy of Country Music Album of the Year Award
Academy of Country Music Entertainer of the Year Award
Academy of Country Music Single of the Year Award
Academy of Country Music Top Male Vocalist Award
Academy of Country Music Video of the Year Award
Academy of Country Music Song of the Year Award
Country Music Association Video of the Year Award

1991

Academy of Country Music Entertainer of the Year Award
Academy of Country Music Top Male Vocalist Award
American Music Award for favorite single
Country Music Association Album of the Year Award
Country Music Association Entertainer of the Year Award
Country Music Association Music Video of the Year Award
Country Music Association Single of the Year Award
Grammy for best male country vocal performance

1992

American Music Award for favorite male artist
American Music Award for favorite album
American Music Award for favorite single
Academy of Country Music Entertainer of the Year Award
Country Music Association Album of the Year Award
Country Music Association Entertainer of the Year Award

1993
American Music Award for favorite male artist
ASCAP Songwriter of the Year Award
Academy of Country Music Entertainer of the Year Award
Academy of Country Music Video of the Year Award

1994
American Music Award for favorite male artist
ASCAP Songwriter of the Year Award
Academy of Country Music Video of the Year Award

1995
American Music Award for favorite male artist

1996
American Music Award for favorite male artist
American Music Award for favorite album

1997
American Music Award for favorite male artist
Country Music Association Entertainer of the Year Award

1998
American Music Award for favorite male artist
Academy of Country Music Entertainer of the Year Award
Academy of Country Music Special Achievement Award
Country Music Association Entertainer of the Year Award
Grammy for best country vocal collaboration

1999
American Music Award for favorite male artist
American Music Award for favorite album

For Further Reading

Paul M. Howey, *Garth Brooks: Chart-Bustin' Country*. New York: Lerner, 1997. Not only provides an interesting overview of the life and music of the artist but also looks at how the music industry works.

Lee Randall, *The Garth Brooks Scrapbook*. New York: Citadel, 1992. A look at the early life and work of Garth Brooks.

Edward Tallman, *Garth Brooks: Straight from the Heart*. New York: Dillon, 1993. A favorable look at Garth Brooks, focusing on his character and artistic independence. Includes color photographs.

Rosemary Wallner, *Garth Brooks: Country Music Star*. New York: Abdo & Daughters, 1993. This thirty-two-page biography provides an easy-to-read look at the life and career of the popular country musician.

Works Consulted

Books

Curtis W. Ellison, *Country Music Culture: From Hard Times to Heaven*. Jackson: University Press of Mississippi, 1995. A detailed account of the rise in popularity of country music from the 1920s to today.

Ralph Emery with Tom Carter, *More Memories*. New York: G. P. Putnam's Sons, 1993. Recollections about the world of country music by the popular host of TNN's *Nashville Now*.

Bruce Feiler, *Dreaming Out Loud: Garth Brooks, Wynonna Judd, Wade Hayes, and the Changing Face of Nashville*. New York: Avon Books, 1998. A look at how country music was transformed from "the voice of a distinct minority: the working-class Southerners" to "the voice of the new American majority."

Rick Mitchell, *Garth Brooks: One of a Kind, Workin' on a Full House*. New York: Simon and Schuster, 1993. A photo essay of the entertainer's rise to stardom, from his youth in Yukon, Oklahoma, to his success in concerts throughout the world.

Edward Morris, *Garth Brooks: Platinum Cowboy*. New York: St. Martin's, 1993. A thorough, detailed account of Brooks's early rise to fame.

Matt O'Meilia, *Garth Brooks: The Road out of Santa Fe*. Norman: University of Oklahoma Press, 1997. A first-person account of the period in Garth Brooks's life just prior to moving to Nashville and becoming the best-selling solo artist of all time.

Periodicals

Associated Press (press release), "Two Cable Channels Ban a Country Music Video," May 5, 1991.

Elizabeth Bland, "Country Classicists," *Time*, September 24, 1990.

Eric Boehlert, "Garth Brooks: Central Park," *Rolling Stone*, September 18, 1997.

Jay Cocks, "Friends in Low Places," *Time*, March 30, 1992.

Anthony DeCurtis, "Ropin' in the Whirlwind," *Rolling Stone*, April 1, 1993.

Christopher John Farley, "Garth Brooks Unplugged," *Time*, August 18, 1997.

Peter Galvin, "Don't Be Fooled by Garth Brooks's Flag-Waving," *Interview*, March 1994.

Edna Gundersen, "Garth Brooks: A Breath of Fresh Air or a Pop Intrusion?" *USA Today*, March 12, 1992.

Robert Hillburn, "The Amazing Garth-O-Matic," *Los Angeles Times*, June 28, 1992.

Jim Jerome, "The New King of Country," *People*, October 7, 1991.

Greg Kot, "Garth Brooks Rolling Along with Winning Ways," *Chicago Tribune*, October 23, 1997.

Mark Lasswell, "Garth Takes Manhattan," *TV Guide*, August 2, 1997.

Marjie McGraw, "Garth Brooks: Hitting 'Em in the Heart," *Saturday Evening Post*, July/August 1992.

Melinda Newman and Edward Morris, "Garth Bows Latest (*Billboard*—Last?) Sets," *Billboard*, September 5, 1992.

Priscilla Painton, "Country Rocks the Boomers," *Time*, March 30, 1992.

People, "Garth Brooks's Black Eye," May 20, 1991.

Neil Pond, "Garth Takes a Bite of the Big Apple," *Country America*, September 1997.

Jane Sanderson, "For Garth Brooks, Country Music's Newest Nova, Nashville Proves Sweeter the Second Time Around," *People*, August 1990.

Tamara Saviano, Wendy Newcomer, and Deborah Barnes, "A Tale of Two Cities on a Night to Remember," *Country Weekly*, October 13, 1998.

Karen Schoemer, "The World According to Garth," *Newsweek*, March 16, 1998.

Jim Sexton, "Garth Brooks Goes Global," *USA Weekend*, December 12, 1995.

Internet Sources

America Online interview with Garth Brooks, September 9, 1994. www.westworld.com/~garthbrk/garth9-9.html.

Country.com, "The Artists: Garth Brooks." www.country.com/ cgi/redirect.cgi?URL=%2Fgen%2Fmusic%2Fartist%2Fgarth -brooks.html.

———, "The History of the *Grand Ole Opry*." www.country. com/music/opry/opry-history-f.html.

Country 105, "Featured Artist: Garth Brooks." www.country 105.com/artistpast/garth1.html.

Encyclopedia of Popular Music, 1989–1998. www.cdnow.com/cgi- bin/mserver/SID=1201610083/pagename=/RP/CDN/FIN D/biography.html/ArtistID=FRN-ENGLAND*TY.

Gary Graff, "Garth Brooks Is Ropin' the Wind and Everything Else," Reuters News Service, May 14, 1998. www. planetgarth.com/gbnews/garth225.shtml.

David Leon Moore, "Brooks a Hit with Padres," *USA Today*, February 26, 1999. www.usatoday.com/sports/ccovfri.htm.

Planet Garth, "The Albums." www.planetgarth.com/gbalbums.

Bob Thomas, "Garth Brooks's TV Special Shows Irish Love for American Country Music," Associated Press, February 27, 1998. www.planetgarth.com/gbnews/garth202.shtml.

Westwood One Entertainment, "The Garth Brooks Story," Planet Garth, July 4, 1996. www.planetgarth.com/gbstory/ gbstory.shtml.

Index

Picture Credits

About the Author

For more than twenty-five years, Jack L. Roberts has worked as an editor and writer of educational materials for elementary and junior high school students and teachers at both the Children's Television Workshop and Scholastic.

In addition, he has written several books for young readers, including a junior high school textbook on computer literacy as well as biographies of President Bill Clinton, South African civil rights leader Nelson Mandela, and U.S. Supreme Court justice Ruth Bader Ginsburg.

This is his third biography for Lucent Books. His other two Lucent titles are *The Importance of Dian Fossey* and *The Importance of Oskar Schindler*.

Roberts lives in Los Angeles and has been a fan of country music even before it was mainstream.